LIVING WITH THE DUTCH

An American Woman Finds Friendship Abroad

Norean Sharpe

This is the 2nd Edition of Living with the Dutch, published by KIT Publishing in 2005.

Published by Central Park South Publishing 2021
www.centralparksouthpublishing.com

Typesetting and e-book formatting services by Victor Marcos

ISBN: 978-1-956452-04-4

This book is dedicated to my children, Katrina and PJ, who have had the patience to live with me, learn from me, and love me.

Acknowledgments

I am indebted to my Dutch neighbors (Marie Louise, William, Machteld, Anne Marie, and Elisabeth), for making my family feel welcome in a foreign land.

I am thankful for the time spent with our friends Triona and Richard, and their shared support and encouragement.

Finally, I am grateful for the talented artists who created the beautiful cover for this 2nd edition, and for the patience of the editors at Central Park South Publishing.

Preface

Writing this story has been a bittersweet journey. The self-exploration has been healing and led to personal growth, although the sharing of private perceptions has also been difficult. I chose to tell my story in the hopes of expanding the expectations and experiences of others living abroad.

While I share the events of travels with my family, the observations I have included here are mine alone. I have attempted to be honest in my impressions of my relationships with both *Nederlanders* and expatriates, yet clearly my perceptions are based on my perspective and the specific interactions that I experienced.

All actions, activities, and conversations in this book did take place – either prior to our move, or while we lived in the Netherlands. However, I may have changed the order of their occurrence or paraphrased the actual conversations, since my memory is not infallible. In addition, between the time of writing and publication, many changes in global relations, security, exchange rates, feminism, adolescent research, and private education will have taken place. Thus, these are my own perceptions of my contact and communication with the Dutch people during the years of my travels in Europe.

Living among a different culture is an invaluable and irreplaceable experience. I am thankful that I was able to grab opportunities to make the most of my time abroad, and I realize that not all travelers are as fortunate. When faced with my next adventure, I remain committed to responding with even more confidence, "Let's go!"

Preface

Herinneringen aan Holland*

Denkend aan Holland
zie ik mooie molens
vlakbij brede autobanen
in een rij staan,
verschilende oude
mooie steden
zoals Amsterdam en Breda
met grote gebouwen
langs de grachten
die door oneindig
laagland gaan;
en aan de kust
hemelsbrede stranden
met blonde kinderen
en poedelnaakte mensen,
blaast een ijskoude wind
de hond van zijn lijn
en de man van zijn fiets,
en de zon schijnt
minder en minder
gedurende de winter,
maar mijn lievelings stad
met smale straten
traag door kleine buurten
en door het centrum gaan,
waar ik woon, graag
en ik ben t'huis
is Den Haag.

Norean Radke Sharpe

---

* This is my updated version of the well-known poem *Denkend aan Holland* by Hendrik Marsman (1899-1945).

Contents

De boog kan niet altijd gespannen zijn.

The bow cannot always be stretched.

Chapter 1

Let's Go!

I never imagined being nurtured in the Netherlands—something I unknowingly needed. With ten years of teaching under my belt, and tenure behind me, I believed I was living the dream of a modern woman. One husband, two children, and three sets of in-laws—who could ask for more? My daily routine offered no clues that an expatriate experience would be enlightening and healing—a dose of medicine for the soul.

Working was my drug of choice. I couldn't get enough. I worked when the sun rose, the moon set, and when most were celebrating the Sabbath. When I wasn't working, I was anxiously awaiting my next fix—my next paper or presentation. I was hooked and gave new meaning to the term 'workaholic.'

Did I work because I had no other source of satisfaction? No. In fact, I had two beautiful children and a loving husband waiting at home. It didn't matter. I started out with the soft stuff—working a few extra hours a week, telling myself it was temporary—just to get myself through the tenure process—and that then I wouldn't need the adrenaline rush anymore. But

I wasn't strong enough. My life became totally consumed by this new, energizing substance, which was motivated by the promise of promotion.

My employer denied any and all responsibility. I was told that I had never learned to "just say no." It was true. The extra committees, classes, students, and advisees were accepted—all without protest or disclaimer. My addiction was the result of my own desire to live in a euphoric and ecstatic state of success—respected by colleagues, demanded by students, and published in prestigious journals. However, I was never aware of the intense side effects of such a commitment to my career. They did not appear in any medical journal.

During the 1990's, women were expected to be everything to everyone—mother, wife, sister, colleague, coach, house manager, and career-climber—and never "let them see you sweat." We were blessed to stand on the shoulders of those women who paved the way before us—but were ill-equipped and unsupported culturally to continue with 80% of the childcare, while striving to achieve personal success and fulfill all future expectations. Most women of a similar age can relate to these diametric demands—as we struggled to put our education to good use and be the generation that shattered our artificial walls and ceilings.

Change was needed to provide a path to regain balance and perspective.

Figuring out what had to change was not easy. Friends gave me advice, but a prescription handed out by others has limited healing power. I did not have the strength to walk away. No one voluntarily places herself in withdrawal. The user must be dealt cards that force her hand—cards which present a clear choice.

This choice came unexpectedly—as most choices do—and was cleverly disguised as an opportunity just tempting enough to consider "going cold turkey." My husband, Peter, was offered an overseas assignment that gave him a long-desired challenge, a well-deserved promotion, and much-needed global experience. What did I think of moving abroad? I didn't need to think. I knew instantly. This was it—my, and our, opportunity to change direction. After all, if my choice was the Betty Ford Clinic for an addiction to work, or a few years exploring Europe, my decision was clear. I said, "Let's go!"

Not only were we to move to Europe, but to Paris: city of lights, champagne and the Champs Elysées. I would learn the nuances of French expressions and the secrets of French chefs. The subtleties of French artists—Renoir, Monet, Degas—would be at my fingertips and become residents of my extended backyard. I signed my children up for French lessons, sought advice on the differences among Parisian *arrondissements*, and bought "self-guided, easy-to-learn" French software. My brothers booked airline tickets to be our first house guests, we reserved two places for our children at the well-known American School in Paris and spent days house hunting in the suburbs of Paris—St. Cloud, Bougival, and Le Vesinet. We were going to be prepared!

Then Peter was required to move early—four months early. I had reluctantly committed to teaching one more semester before my leave, so I remained behind in the U.S. with the kids. As a result, I was in complete charge of packing up the house, organizing all necessary papers from the public school system, and visiting (and re-visiting for endless vaccinations) our local veterinarian to update the medical status of our black Labrador Retriever.

No problem. An additional semester in the States would ease my transition.(I was naive and soon discovered that letting go of my friends, students, and courses week-by-week was like slowly scratching a blackboard). No problem, an additional four months would provide much-needed preparation time. I could buy guidebooks, plan trips, schedule tours of the new school for the children, and find renters for our home. In addition, French was difficult to learn in eight weeks—

sixteen more would give me the time to listen to all eighteen lessons. I would soon be bilingual!

No problem. My husband would need time to line up European psychiatrists for my certain and eventual inability to cope with withdrawal and the move abroad. After teaching for over ten years, my colleagues and close friends had doubts I would be able to adjust. No schedule. No deadlines. No students. No committees. No colleagues. No life!

They all predicted that one of three things would happen: one, I would return *immediately* to my teaching position; two, I would apply to teach at multiple European universities and see nothing beyond the inside of a commuter rail; or three, I would *eventually* return home alone—without husband and children, who had decided to remain expatriates forever. This was not the kind of support I envisioned and I soon began plotting a plea of temporary insanity to explain my behavior, should any of their predictions come true.

During the months following our decision, many of my female colleagues eyed me with disbelief—I was, after all, giving up what I had worked so hard for: recognition in a male-dominated discipline. My friends were doubtful, to say the least. While they were envious at my prospect of not having to work weekends and late nights, they also assumed I would immediately conduct a job search. They, just like I, believed that my identity was more dependent on *what I did*, than on *who I was*.

My own extended family was also concerned about this change in my life. They were blind to the worsening physical ailments brought on by the daily tolls of my inability to find a "work-life balance." They believed what we wanted them to believe. They knew what we told them.

While my mom did not know the details of my day-to-day struggles, she knew for sure that I had never followed *any* man *anywhere* in my life. My husband and I had lived apart for over half of our fifteen-year marriage to achieve a two-career partnership. Why was I now changing my strategy? Why would I now follow a man—despite the fact that this man was my husband—halfway around the world?

Whatever others knew or believed, my husband and I agreed—this change was necessary. It was with this decisiveness that I walked away from an all-consuming career and packed our belongings for eventual delivery to the port of Le Havre in France.

De laatste loodjes wegen het zwaarst.

It is the last straw that breaks the camel's back.

Chapter 2

Moving Day Madness

We were confident that our move overseas would proceed smoothly with no surprises. Then, shortly before moving day, my husband called from Paris.

Peter: *The good news is that I have made a verbal agreement with Madame DuPres on the house in St. Cloud.*

Me: *Wonderful!*

Peter: *The not-so-good news is that my job is not challenging.*

Me: *What do you mean?*

Peter: *I am not being intellectually challenged.*

Me: *Isn't learning French intellectually challenging?*

Peter: *My technical expertise is under-utilized.*

Me: *But didn't you accept the position to network?*

Peter: *Well...yes.*

Me: *Are your colleagues enjoyable to work with?*

Peter: *Oh, they are great and we have weekly occasions to drink champagne—you know, every time someone's poodle has a birthday.*

Me: *Then what is the problem? — besides the fact that you have far too many office parties!*

Peter: *I have been offered another opportunity to manage global accounts.*

Me: *Great! So, what is the problem?*

Peter: *Well…*

Me: *Well, what? Where is this new opportunity?*

Peter: *The Netherlands*

Me: *Where?!*

No problem. We bid adieu to the city of cognac and said *goede middag* to the city of Haagse Hopjes. We relabeled our boxes "Rotterdam" and phoned the movers. After all, there were good international schools in The Hague. Surely, they would have space available...to our amazement and disappointment, the schools were full.

No problem. A quick trip to the Netherlands and hours later Peter signed papers for our new home (sight unseen by me). So what if we weren't moving to Paris. So what if we didn't speak Dutch. So what if our children faced the prospect of being home-schooled by their mother—a fate worse than death! So what if we left one angry French landlady and two grateful school children on a long waiting list in St. Cloud. So what if my brother cancelled his tickets for next spring and told us that moving from Paris to The Hague was like moving from Boston to Cincinnati!

Our first shipment was picked up on the eve of Thanksgiving to allow the necessary travel time (at least six weeks!) to the port of Rotterdam. Clearly, I did not cook a turkey the next day. The absence of tables and chairs would have forced us to eat our drumsticks Japanese style and this seemed unpatriotic, not to mention uncomfortable.

Fate in hand, we were only too happy to escape to the grandparents for our holiday meal. Besides, our children had grown tired of drooling when Dad carved the turkey only to discover tiny bags of unidentified parts inside. (I think our son believed for years that turkeys waddled around because the wads of plastic in them restricted them from further movement.) Admittedly, I never claimed to be a cook when I got married—and thank goodness the Dutch don't eat much turkey.

The brilliance of our idea to ship two-thirds of our goods early was that we would have access to our furniture when we arrived in Holland; ostensibly to prevent the children from sleeping on the floor and to aid in our transition. Our intentions were good, but our expectations were naïve. We quickly discovered that the signature from each and every government official in the Netherlands—all 500 of them—was required to retrieve our furniture from customs. Our goods were held captive for what seemed like an even heavier ransom of five forms of identification, four birth certificates, three verifications of residence, two large sums of money, and one letter from my husband's employer.

Unaware of future furniture captivity, and having shipped all of our worldly goods on the slow boat to Holland, we spent our final weeks in the States without sofas, chairs, beds, dishes or silverware. The children and I kept our spirits up (Peter remained in Paris on assignment) by pretending that it was the mother of all sleepovers—after all, we still had a TV, stereo, popcorn popper, and coffee maker—what more could we ask for?

Air-shipment boxes containing those essential items that we were convinced we couldn't live without, like Legos and favorite stuffed animals, were picked up just prior to our departure. Finally, our domestic storage container for the remaining one-third of our goods that we would leave behind was picked up on the day after Christmas. Looking back on the plan of attack, I would still agree to live months without beds, bowls and blankets, but I would never again move during the holidays. While we had the element of surprise and the lack of time to over-analyze and lose courage, it was difficult to find time to 'deck the halls' and feel any 'joy to the world.'

Christmas week found me still computing final grades (no different from prior years), and packing up my soon-to-be-ex-office. When the last crew of movers arrived, they were dismayed at our state of *untidiness*! The floors were littered with half-empty boxes; mattresses were still wrapped in sheets (we should have slept at a hotel); wet clothes sat in the washing machine (ultimately forgotten); unclean carpets covered the floors (American dirt was indeed transported to Holland); and curtains still hung on the windows. I guess we should have paraded naked in front of the neighbors for six weeks.

Tension mounted. I blamed Peter for not participating, as he was in Paris until December 21st, he "chided" me for not beginning the packing sooner, the kids complained about leaving their friends, our Labrador wandered aimlessly among the boxes trying to sniff out the reason for all this upheaval, and the movers worked furiously for days—convinced we were all mad.

At the end of the invasion and subsequent retreat of packers, wrappers, tapers and truckers, we stood in our empty house with our realtor. She, too, was amazed at the state of our disarray and estimated the cost of having the house thoroughly cleaned—perhaps fumigated—prior to the arrival of the new tenants. (The children could not bear the sale of our home.) We settled last-minute details and tried to dispel feelings of doubt as we stood in the empty rooms among reams of movers' inventory sheets (all 27 pages); phone bills (still to pay or cancel); rental contracts (still to sign); car titles (but not the ones we needed); and hopefully, our airline tickets somewhere at the bottom of the pile.

A moment of sentimentality was short-lived. As all true procrastinators, we had left too much for the final day—whatever happened to the 36-hour day? Either Peter thought *I* would handle these details, or I thought *he* would take care of them, or neither of us had time to think. We still needed to finalize the sale of our Jeep, deliver our second car to storage, visit the bank, drop off boxes to Good Will, leave our forwarding address at the post office, phone the phone company, and visit with far too many friends for a promised farewell drink. Panic set in. It was off to the races, if we were to make our late-night flight.

Four hours later, we—four people lugging a 100-pound Labrador in his travel cage—raced (OK, limped) into the KLM terminal of Logan Airport. Whatever feelings we had that our pooch would have no companionship on the plane were left at the door. The terminal was filled with canine yappers—dogs the size of large cats all loudly yelping in their own padded cells. Of course, *our* beloved Mickie was perfectly behaved. Was this due to him being a frequent traveler? No, it was thanks to those sleeping pills from the vet! After a show of tickets, proof of injections, and the requisite letters with six signatures—all for the dog—man's best friend was promised a warm passage to Holland. Ironically, we, on the other hand, passed inspection much more quickly. With only our passports in hand and a wave from the airline attendants, we embarked on what was to become a life-changing journey.

Achter de wolken schijnt de zon.

Every cloud has a silver lining.

Chapter 3

Weathering the Winter

We arrived in the Netherlands just in time to celebrate the New Year. Our furniture was being held hostage, while we "camped" out at a palace in the seaside town of Scheveningen. Life was relatively good. The back of our hotel opened onto the beachfront boardwalk and our room overlooked the Noordzee where the arctic air was biting, yet beckoning. It came as no surprise to us that in the latter part of the nineteenth century, our hotel had been used as a place for the local Dutch to clear their lungs and convalesce.

Looking back on our arrival in the Netherlands that bitter winter, I'm not sure what I expected. What I remember is entering a foggy and misty scene that gave the surroundings an eerie, almost mystical quality. Each day of our first two months, we had a mere six hours of daylight, with an emphasis on "day" and not "light," and a continuous stream of rain. The sky resembled a dull shade of gray. I recall repeatedly describing the weather during these early months as dark, dank and dreary. No wonder many of the paintings of Rembrandt and Vermeer were dark. It was all they knew.

The Netherlands is a relatively small, flat and low-lying country with expertise in managing the sea.

The Netherlands is home to approximately 17 million people and is known as the low country. In fact, its name in both Dutch and French (*Nederland* and *Pays Bas)* means 'low land,' with estimates placing nearly one-third of the country below sea-level. One only needs to visit the many canals, locks, and dykes for this realization to sink in. Even the main airport, Schiphol, is built on reclaimed land—what used to be the *Haarlemmermeer*, or Haarlem Lake, and is now one of the busiest airports in Europe. Several books on the geography, culture and history of this resourceful nation provide a perspective on the Dutch traditions, policies and socialistic leanings. [1–5]

Other books have been written that focus exclusively on providing advice for expatriates settling in the Netherlands. These how-to-live-and-cope books contain essential details of adjusting to everyday life, as well as important rules and regulations. At least one of these guidebooks is a must-read for any expatriate who plans to take up residence—temporary or permanent—in the Netherlands.[6-10]

Suffice it to say that it's not that life in the Netherlands is more difficult; it's just different. For example, I needed to learn to pay my parking ticket *prior* to getting in my car at a parking garage—or I was the source of a long line of Nederlanders who became unpleasant when I realized the machine at the exit required a pre-paid ticket! (While this parking arrangement is more common in the States now, I had never seen it prior to our move overseas.)

On a side note, while many use the terms "Holland" and "Netherlands" interchangeably, Holland is actually an area within the Netherlands, comprised of two provinces: Noord-Holland and Zuid-Holland. These two provinces, out of a total of 12, contain the country's three largest cities (Amsterdam, Rotterdam, and Den Haag) and over one-third of the national population, thus forming the base of the national economy. Hence, many people have grown accustomed to referring to the larger area as Holland.

While the sense of dreariness we felt in our new country was a real and natural result of the lack of sunshine, this impression was not reflective of the Dutch people. The silver lining of the gray skies and chilly climate of this low land turned out to be the warmth of its inhabitants—who are fun-loving people, despite the unfriendly skies. Perhaps they have developed an alternative resource to release the hormones that stimulate our mood, or perhaps this explains the Red-light District!

Appreciating its value, the locals worshiped each glimpse of the warmth and glow of the sun—no matter how faint. We observed families erupting from their houses and workers racing from their offices to soak up every drop of the healing rays. They appeared in hoards, all with multiple children, to battle the 50-km/hr winds off the Noordzee and to stroll along the beach. Since the beach was a ten-minute bike ride from Den Haag, the golden orb may have disappeared by the time they reached the sand but it didn't matter, because a 10-minute bike ride to a Nederlander is equivalent to a 10-second walk to an American.

All winter long, the beachfront was jammed with families on the weekends. Each family had several children, all below the age of eight, and at least two dogs—or so it seemed. The children were encouraged to run, skip, scream and play at the water's edge, which was reported to have sub-zero temperatures. Dogs ran wild—no leashes and sometimes no owners in sight. Such activity seemed unusual to us during a period when most Americans are skiing or snowboarding. However, Den Haag seldom gets snow, and the temperature rarely drops below 40° F during the winter. Moreover, if the sun is ever shining, it is cause for celebration regardless of the time of year.

The beach in Scheveningen is a unique place to visit because of the scenery—besides the families frolicking in the bitter cold. We became aware of just how unique it is one warm day after cycling to the beach on a *fietspad* that delivered us to the northern end of the town's boardwalk. Excited to feel the sand between our toes, we unloaded our saddlebags and ran to the beach, only to discover that we were overdressed. This particular bike path was a direct route to the free and progressive section of the beach; otherwise known as the nude beach.

Although our neighbors who were concerned about our American sensitivities had forewarned us, we had not prepared our children for the occasion. Thus, they were spontaneously introduced to a local custom as an assembly of exposed and mostly older locals strolled by. While long past their prime in fitness, they seemed more than comfortable with their own bare skin, imperfections and all.

At first, our children asked to relocate to a different stretch of sand and adamantly refused to either remove their clothes or be the only ones on the beach in a swimsuit. We explained that we had no intention of asking them to do anything that would make them uncomfortable. Soon after first satisfying their wide-eyed curiosity, they realized that their own state of dress did not bother the locals, and they resumed building their sand castle. Eventually the sunbathers paled in comparison to the rest of the scenery—although the locals were anything but pale.

As months of rainy Nordic weather passed, we began to appreciate the behavior of the locals frolicking at the edge of the North Pole to feel a fleeting glimpse of warmth. The first view of sunshine prompted alert calls both to Peter at work and to our neighbors. Meetings were missed and dishes were dropped as we raced to the great outdoors. We became staunch members of the "Beachcombers-with-a-Dog-and-Young-Kids Society" and faithfully joined this hearty and healthy crowd each weekend at Scheveningen Strand. We politely refused, however, to join the "Let's-Jump-in-the-Noordzee-Society" on New Year's Day, or the "Let's-Sunbathe-Nude-Society" on all other days.

All winter and spring, we walked the beach among the scarf-swaddled couples, bands of youngsters, and packs of pooches, in a state of culture shock. Between gasps of *ijskoud* air and clutches to keep our warmest winter coat collars closed against the Noordzee gales, we appreciated the feeling of being together, particularly since we had long lost all other feeling and numbness had taken over our extremities, a feeling I cannot remember having in a long time...no, not the numbness—the closeness.

It was a family feeling that grew—a feeling that we were in this adventure together and if we were going to succeed in adopting our new country, we needed to depend on each other. No, this was not the Swiss Family Robinson, but a new period of exploration for the Dutch "Familie van Sharpe."

NOTES

Chapter 3: Weathering the Winter

1. Blom, J.C.H. and E. Lamberts (eds.) (1999), *History of the Low Countries*, New York: Berghahn Books.
2. van der Horst, Han (2001), *The Low Sky: Understanding the Dutch* (5th Edition), Schiedam: Scriptum Publishers.
3. Isreal, Jonathan (1998), *The Dutch Republic: Its Rise, Greatness, and Fall 1477-1806, Oxford: Oxford Press.*
4. De Jong, L. (2002), *The Collapse of a Colonial Society*, Leiden: KITLV Press.
5. Schama, Simon (1997), *The Embarrassment of Riches*, New York: Random House.
6. American Women's Club of The Hague (1998), *At Home in Holland* (8th edition), Delft: Eburon Publishers.
7. Coates, Ben (2017), *Why the Dutch are Different: A Journey into the Hidden Heart of the Netherlands*, London: Nicholas Brealey Publishing.
8. Janin, Hunt (1998), *Culture Shock: A Guide to Customs and Etiquette*, Singapore: Times Editions Pte Ltd.
9. Vossestein, J. (1997), *Dealing with the Dutch*, Amsterdam: KIT Publishers.
10. White, Colin and Laurie Boucke (2017), *The UnDutchables*, Lafayette, CO: White-Boucke Publishing, Inc.

Beter een goede buur dan een verre vriend.

It is better to have a good neighbor than a faraway friend.

Chapter 4

Meeting the Neighbors

Our relationship with the Dutch began with flying notes. On the second day in our new home in The Hague after finally freeing our belongings from bondage, small pieces of paper started appearing on the floor of our foyer. These notes contained words scrawled in a mixture of Dutch and English and arrived via the mail slot in our front door. A short period of sleuthing on our parts revealed the sender: an impish figure with such angelic Shirley-temple gold curls that we thought perhaps we were having hallucinations from delayed jet lag.

These notes explained that three Dutch girls, ages 7, 9, and 12, lived next door and wanted to meet us. Since our children at the time were 9 and 12, we thought we were either the luckiest expatriates in The Hague, or part of a cruel joke played on over-stressed, homebound mothers. The next time paper flew into our home, we caught it midair and flung the door open just in time to surprise two girls, staring at us with mischievous guilt. As they turned to make their getaway, a tall woman appeared on our stoop and introduced herself in flawless British English as Marie Louise.

She was our neighbor, and wanted to welcome us to the neighborhood. Did we need anything? Where were we from? What brought us to the Netherlands? How long would we stay? Forget the guidebooks that say Dutch people are difficult to meet!

Thus began a relationship that grew over a period of twenty months into a nurturing and mutual friendship. I would discover with Louise's help, that the most pleasant and efficient way to view the local language, culture, and politics is through the lens of a native *Nederlander*. Daily conversations were shared over coffee. Confessions about motherhood poured out with cocktails. Heated political debates carried on into the pre-dawn hours. And all were carried out in our own "perfected" mix of English and Dutch. Yes, I learned the local language, after much intense study and most likely embarrassment at my own expense.

These were the threads that bound us together: two women who were simply doing their best to raise their children. Our two homelands had a rich history for separate ideas on socialism versus capitalism; neutrality versus isolationism; and atheism versus Catholicism. Yet, our experiences as women, wives and mothers displaced all differences and provided our own source of camaraderie.

Perhaps we should not have been surprised by this alliance between a *Nederlander* and a *New Englander*. After all, we share a common heritage and a common search for individualism and independent thought. In fact, parts of modern-day democracy can trace its origins to the separatists, or Pilgrims, who learned it from the Dutch, at least according to theory.

In 1608, King James I was the head of the Anglican Church in England. An individual who enjoyed power and control, he was known for his persecution of those that had different religious ideas, especially those that wanted to officially separate from the King's Church. Most Puritans believed in reform by increasing their power in the English government, but a small group, the separatists, believed that the only solution was a total separation from the Anglican establishment.[1] After years of suffering under English rules and restrictions, these separatists decided to move to Amsterdam in search of religious freedom and a more tolerant government. The following year, after a disagreement over internal affairs, a group of these separatists moved west to the town of Leiden (often referred to as Leyden), just north of The Hague, and settled near the *Pieterskerk*.[2]

Here, for eleven years, these separatists worshipped freely, studied the local language, learned the Dutch trades, and adopted many of the Dutch customs. (Note that during these same years, Rembrandt was living in Leiden and developing his talent as an artist, although it is not known whether or not he interacted directly with the Puritans.) While this was a period of peace but not prosperity, absorption of their families into the Dutch culture became a growing concern—especially since the Dutch believed that merriment on Sundays was acceptable, a trait frowned upon by the faithful separatists.[3] (Yes, it's true, the Dutch have had their free-spirit, peace-loving and party reputation since the seventeenth century.)

In addition to the poor economic outlook and a loss of more conservative Puritan traditions, these separatists feared a potential return to war, since the existing truce with Spain was nearing an end. Thus, despite several years of peaceful coexistence, it was the harshness of the land and economy, the increasing restrictions on religious practices, the concern over Dutch morals and merrymaking, and the threat of renewed occupation by Spain that prompted a large group of separatists to search for a new home.[4]

The religious leaders initially considered moving to Jamestown, Virginia, but were concerned about being persecuted by fellow colonists. Instead, they negotiated with James I to occupy unsettled territory owned by the Virginia Company.[5] In return for seven years' labor, each colonist, including children, earned shares in a joint-stock association. Although the separatists were not satisfied with the terms of travel, they chose this option over an offer by the Dutch for a funded settlement in New Amsterdam which would have placed Plymouth Rock on Staten Island, instead of Massachusetts. [5] After boarding a ship at Delfshaven, a harbor town south of Leiden, for Southampton, England, this group of enterprising individuals, now considered Pilgrims, eventually left Plymouth, England aboard the Mayflower in 1620 bound for America.

Unbeknownst to most people even today, these Pilgrims brought many Dutch customs that they found useful with them; the most well-known of these being the American celebration of Thanksgiving. Some argue that this traditional feast can trace its origins back to the *Pieterskerk*, where an annual service of thanks celebrates the liberation from the siege of 1574 through the sharing of *hutspot* (a hearty winter stew) and herring to commemorate the delivery of food to a starving city.[2] I, for one, am appreciative that the American Pilgrims chose *not* to include herring in their celebration.

Secondly, the Pilgrims are thought by many to have brought the practice of civil marriage with them. During the sixteenth and seventeenth centuries, since a large number of Dutch citizens could not be wed in a church, as they were Roman Catholics, the government allowed justices to marry non-members of the state church. Because a marriage conducted outside the walls of a church was typically not permitted, the legalization of civil marriages was an enormous step towards the acceptance of multiple religions. The Pilgrims did not forget this upon their arrival in America.[2]

Finally, even in the sixteenth century, the structure of city government in Holland depended on elected officials. Leiden was composed of districts, each with a district governor, charged with managing taxes and welfare. The Pilgrims lived under this system of government from 1609 until as late as 1629 for the late-arrivers, and used aspects of the elected government concept in creating their Mayflower Compact.[2, 6]

While not widely known, a long-standing debate was carried on in the United States, often publicly, into the middle of the nineteenth century about whether the influence of Dutch society on the Puritans was positive or negative—as witnessed by their solid example of a municipal republican government, or their subtle, yet degrading, outlook on morality.

In contrast to the Pilgrims, who adopted and transported the Dutch customs, whether beneficial or detrimental, to the shores of New England, other separatists decided to remain behind in Holland. This group settled permanently in Leiden, becoming absorbed into, and contributing to, the Dutch culture in the area. Thus, I deduced that both my Dutch neighbor and I have the same Pilgrim individualist, independent blood running through our veins. I like to tell myself that this may partially explain the immediate connection between two apparently diverse and dissimilar women—one raised in southern Netherlands and the other raised in southern New England.

Soon after the introduction instigated by my neighbor's daughters, Marie Louise and I, in typical Dutch style, began to cycle to town. We shared childhood stories and explored the differences between our opportunities as a *huisvrouw* and *moeder*. For example, daycare and after-school programs are less common in the Netherlands than in the U.S., and this limited availability of affordable childcare, combined with the Dutch emphasis on family life, often inhibits women from pursuing careers. According to Hunt Janin in *Culture Shock*, relatively few mothers worked full-time in the Netherlands in the 1990's compared to other developed countries, although this percentage is growing.[7] Han van der Horst in *The Low Sky* writes about feminist waves and a growing trend of Dutch mothers entering the workforce after their children have become independent.[8] As a testimony to this change, my Dutch neighbor had two sisters with careers; one as a professor in philosophy and the second as a family doctor with three children of her own.

Many of the Dutch are well-educated and my neighbor, with a degree from Universiteit Groningen, was no exception. Our conversations may not have been typical for two nearly middle-aged women; she had a penchant for debating the policies of each of the U.S. political parties to which I often obliged over lunch in her rose garden. Our homes were classic Dutch side-by-side, four-storied brick townhouses, one-room wide and two rooms deep, each with its own enormous garden and patio and an easy walk from the city center.

Marie Louise's knowledge of politicians from both major parties in the U.S. was impressive. Explaining the logic of our electoral system was probably my biggest challenge, since the impact of votes depends on the size of the state. I quickly learned that international politics was more likely to be front-page news in the Netherlands than in the United States. In addition, the Dutch receive signals for radio and television from at least four other countries, so Louise was well-informed, as are the majority of the *Nederlanders*.

Our most stimulating discussions often took place during afternoon cycle rides, as we dodged traffic and fellow bicyclists. I recall one occasion when Louise had difficulty understanding the merits of the U.S. clinging to the death penalty, while at the same time opposing euthanasia, a hypocritical viewpoint from her perspective. A challenging defense for me, particularly as we tried to avoid the onslaught of everything else on wheels: cars, trucks, motorbikes, and other cyclists deep in their own arguments!

Over time, the conversations became more complex and controversial as we contested our countries' disparate views on crime and punishment, with the Dutch having legalized "soft" drugs, permitting women to practice prostitution as "entrepreneurs," and defending rehabilitation over incarceration. Besides these issues, the Dutch were early adopters of legalizing the growing of marijuana for a limited number of farmers to sell it for medicinal purposes, which at the time, was a shocking concept for Americans. (We thought all the greenhouses in Holland contained tulips.)

Fond of focusing on the perils and privileges of liberal access to the popular fragrant weed, it was evident from our strolls through the city center that this drug was widely available and frequently used (and they did inhale) among individuals of all ages. Indeed, my shock must have been evident when I was offered a mug of warm milk one evening as a panacea for cramps, and I realized that it did not get its green color from mint leaves.

Rarely could we resist resuming our friendly debates on differences in ideologies, as anything was fair game, over *jenever*—the Dutch version of gin, served ice cold in small quantities if one wanted to win the debate. These musings on the differences between 'us,' who considered ourselves staunch individualists, and 'them,' who proudly defended their Dutch *Koningin* as well as their progressive socialistic views, often lasted until dawn. Fortunately, we had no sense of time, since the winter days were as dark as night.

Both Janin in *Culture Shock*[7] and van der Horst in *The Low Sky*[8] attempt to relay the importance of *gezelligheid*—a Dutch word that defies translation, but represents coziness, togetherness and comfort, as well as an atmosphere of communication, congeniality and collegiality. My neighbor typically used this word to refer to our intimate gatherings, and these are the moments that my husband and I cherished the most during our many months in Holland. Nothing could compare to sparring with new-found friends in a city where decent French wines cost less than $6.00 a bottle and Cuban cigars were imported legally.

Not surprisingly, these conversations took place in English, out of necessity. Although I was studying Dutch, my husband was more focused on learning French since he worked for a French firm, and our neighbors enjoyed practicing their second language. I was impressed with the scope of their knowledge of English idioms and it motivated me to improve my guttural accent, so I practiced whenever I got the chance. Even random people on the street became the benefactors of my efforts.

The strong linguistic element of the Dutch education system was clearly evident as we discovered that many of the locals spoke not only English, but French, German and often Italian as well. Louise speaks four languages; her English is flawless and her French and Italian are sufficient to order all necessities for a full meal at the market in Bordeaux or Tuscany. It is true that many Europeans speak multiple languages out of necessity; our Alpine ski guides all spoke at least *five* languages. However, this move abroad was beginning to make me feel inadequate. My Dutch was on training wheels and my German was rusty, and I found myself wishing that I hadn't returned all those French lessons.

In February, we decided to accept my neighbor's invitation to accompany her family on an extended weekend in Belgium with her academic, provocative sister and her eccentric *Tante* Mieke. What a combination. We were not sure whether we learned more from the sister Angela, who gave us home-brewed medicine for our dog's arthritis (no—it was not green), or from Tante Mieke, whose memory was better than mine. After escaping a fate of frozen cadavers by surviving a search for petrol for 50 kilometers with only 0.001 liters in the tank (Germans aren't kidding when they say their Opels are energy efficient!), we finally arrived at a cottage deep in the Ardennes, an area known for its snowy and bitter winters.

The 200-year-old *huisje* was cozy and comfortable, as long as we used all three eiderdown quilts and slept together in one bed, and the house turned out to be historic for reasons beyond its age. In the extraordinarily harsh winter of 1945, General Patton had used the area as a resting point and as a location for giving orders to his troops during World War II. The black and white photograph on the wall documenting this event revealed tired, drawn and weary faces, surrounded by mounds of snow in the backyard of the cottage.

At the time, villages in the Ardennes formed the epicenter of The Battle of the Bulge, and the entire area was shrouded in shrapnel with soldiers running from foxhole to foxhole. Today, the area is scattered with memorials and monuments to those who fought so bravely in what many consider to be the turning point of the War. We walked among the dense hedgerows, now made famous by cinematography in war films, and visited local grave markers.

Following this visit to the Ardennes, the topic of the War crept into many of our conversations and activities in The Hague. It was clear that the impact of this historical event, while occurring nearly sixty years ago, had left a lasting impact on the inhabitants of this small country—so small that it took Hitler only five days to gain control. I would learn more about the depth of this impact on my future visits to Haarlem, Amsterdam, and to Louise's hometown of Nijmegen.

As a result of my rare relationship with a Dutch *vrouw*, I was able to drink in, share in, and participate in daily life in the Netherlands—not as a tourist, but as a resident—and my observations and experiences subsequently changed how I lived day-to-day, how I treated others, and how I viewed myself.

NOTES

Chapter 4: Meeting the Neighbors

1. Labaree, Benjamin, W. (1979), *Colonial Massachusetts—A History*, New York: KTO Press, p. 18.
2. Details of the Pilgrim's time in Leiden can be found in The Pilgrim Archives, maintained by The Netherlands at: *http://www.pilgrimarchives.nl.*
3. Colby, Jean Poindexter (1970), *Plimoth Plantation Then and Now*, New York: Hastings House Publishers, p. 24-25.
4. Deetz, James and Patricia Deetz (2000), *The Times of Their Lives: Life, Love, and Death in Plymouth Colony*, New York: W.H. Freeman and Company, pp. 33-35.
5. Labaree, p. 25.
6. Seelye, John (1998), *Memory's Nation—The Place of Plymouth Rock*, Chapel Hill, NC: The University of North Carolina Press, pp. 490-491.
7. Janin, Hunt (1998), *Culture Shock: A Guide to Customs and Etiquette*, Singapore: Times Editions Pte Ltd.
8. van der Horst, Han (2001), *The Low Sky: Understanding the Dutch* (5th Edition), Schiedam: Scriptum Publishers.

U moet niet alle praatjes geloven.

Don’t believe all that is told.

Chapter 5

Learning the Language and Culture

Our observations of the Dutch culture were unexpected, even though we had done due diligence by reading the requisite travel guides.[1-3] According to Hunt Janin in *Culture Shock*, the Dutch think of themselves as "an egalitarian, practical, well-organized people who value privacy and self-control."[1] These are common descriptions of the inhabitants of the Low Countries. In fact, the Royal Tropical Institute in Amsterdam, a source of knowledge on various cultures, has identified five traits of the Dutch people: egalitarian, utilitarian, organized, trade-oriented, and privacy-minded. The strong belief of the Dutch in social equality, and the comprehensive social safety net provided by their welfare system has created a society with one of the lowest rates of poverty in the world. In addition, their practice of normalization and tolerance has generated an environment of mutual respect for individual differences, and minimized differences in monetary wealth of its inhabitants.

Both Janin and Han van der Horst stress the impact and scars of World War II; of multiple, devastating floods (in 1953, and more recently in 1995); and of the activist movement in the 1960s, which led to the decline of "pillarization" in Dutch society.[1, 2] The Dutch people responded to each of these events with their traditional attributes of practicality and efficiency and rebuilt their infrastructure with hard work, persistence and a Calvinistic work ethic.

After reading these descriptions, we felt we could adapt well during our stay in the Netherlands. After all, the concept of equality sounded noble and not un-American, and privacy sounded reasonable, since I wasn't planning on being a nosy neighbor. We would be respectful of others, mind our own business, and obey the laws. We were prepared.

It was not the written words or obvious manner, we soon discovered, that presided over every-day life in Holland, but rather the *un*written codes of communication and behavior among the Dutch people. These took time to learn first-hand and, throughout our experiences, we learned to accept the unexpected and live with the element of surprise.

It soon became clear that we were *un*prepared for the scope of our daily discoveries of the approach of the Dutch people and the atmosphere of a Dutch city. I wish I could have bottled the fragrance of daily-cut Dutch flowers, the cold salty sea air off the Noordzee, and the pungent odor of soft cheese at the local shop on the *Bankastraat* (although I'm not sure the Limburg perfume would have sold). Instead, I have had to rely on memory and continued conversations with my *Nederlandse vrienden.* Here, I try to convey our expatriate experiences through observations of the Dutch way of life—both the routine and the extraordinary.

Although many Netherlanders speak English, all paperwork is in Dutch, so learn the language.

Prior to my arrival here in Holland, everyone—and I mean everyone, including realtors, academics, and family members who had traveled to Amsterdam—told us: "Don't worry. You won't need to learn Dutch. Everyone speaks English there." Well, yes and no.

Our observation is that *visiting* a country and *residing* in a country produce two radically different experiences. First, there is the obvious. After a few weeks, hotel living becomes impractical, eating out becomes expensive, and speaking only with family members becomes lonely. Conversing with yourself can help, but this tends to produce odd stares, whereby I often pretended I was scolding the dog.

Thus, we needed a house, preferably with a fully equipped kitchen. For this purpose, along with finding schools for the children, my husband's company provided us with a relocation consultant. Our consultant was an American who was married to a Dutchman, and completely bilingual—an essential aspect of the position that we soon came to depend on, since she became our voice during those early weeks.

In addition to the obvious difference from a temporary stay of even up to several months, are the subtle necessities of becoming a "resident" of a foreign country. Besides assisting us with house hunting and lease negotiation, the consultant enabled us to successfully obtain telephone service, cable TV connection (with the evening news in five languages), automobile parking permits, local bank accounts, police paperwork for *buitenlanders* and customs documents. All paperwork for these transactions was in—you guessed it—Dutch. While this should *not* have been surprising, it was naively unexpected. Moving is difficult enough without the handicap of not being able to read any of the paperwork you are signing.

Nevertheless, it is true that many professionals with whom we conducted business spoke English. The most fluent of these were our banker and car salesman—what this says about the economic wisdom of the Dutch is clear, but we never did understand *all* the controls in our car, since the manuals were only in Dutch and German. However, if we needed assistance—which was often—we discovered that not as many telephone operators were qualified to assist English-speaking customers. This meant more time spent on hold and frequent requests to clearly state our concerns in writing. Automated recordings were a complete mystery to me, and I struggled to learn when and why to press "2" or "3" after the beep (*twee of drie na de pieptonen*) when trying to get the local cinema schedule or find out when my mother's plane was due to arrive. (Of course, the internet has made daily living much easier with schedules, menus, and directions at our fingertips.)

The degree of fluency varies widely among *Nederlanders.* For example, I discovered that the frequent visits arranged by our landlady from painters, plumbers, plasterers and stone-layers went more smoothly once I learned to prattle away in the local tongue. In addition, my new fluency came in handy in negotiating the cost of the stains left by our dog with the landlady, whose English was minimal.

Besides decreasing my frustrating time spent on hold, as well as actually comprehending the taped messages while waiting, learning the native language eased my ability to participate in even the simplest transactions. These included daily functions such as buying *bruinbrood*, *melk*, *kaas*, or *bloemen* at the local *winkels*.

And I did indeed purchase flowers daily, since *tulpen* were fresh and cheap. (A far cry from the 16th century when individual bulbs were sold as stock with a price as high as 1000 guilders per bulb!) Besides these daily needs, knowing Dutch also eased my ability to mail the occasional package at the local *postkantoor*, hire a local caterer (who only spoke French and Dutch), and visit the local *dierenarts*—which was frequent, since by now our dog was age 91 in "people years." Each of these activities became less of a chore, and more of an opportunity to learn more about the *Nederlandse samenleving* (Dutch society), as I conversed with Willi at the local *bloemenwinkel*, Wanda at the corner *Italiaanse winkel*, and the entire family who served me weekly food *te meenemen* at the *Blauwe Lotus*—the neighborhood Indonesian Restaurant.

In addition, emergency visits to the local *tandarts*—particularly when my son cracked his teeth at a local fair—were less stressful because I could communicate with the person holding the syringe and scalpel. (Warning:

the Netherlands does *not* require the same safety standards on carnival bumper cars as the United States.) More importantly, when our dentist brilliantly rebuilt two new front teeth for our son, I was able to clearly express my gratitude—in her own language.

While most *Nederlanders* know how to speak English well, many still prefer to speak in their native tongue. Private conversations, weather reports, traffic reports, local newspapers, advertisements and written data (including all bottles, packages, and food labels) are in Dutch, of course. Thus, unless a *buitenlander* finds a life of isolationism attractive, the decision to learn the local language is a given. So, I signed up for a local course, bought the books and, at the age of 40, became a student again.

As a result of learning *Nederlands*, my relationship with Louise was able to grow beyond the stiff politeness of cut flowers into a blooming friendship—like the climbing roses on her front trellis. Louise assisted my ailing translation skills and most likely rescued me from withering in a Dutch prison—by interpreting many a letter from the *politie*—typically a request for more paperwork to be completed for yet another signed, witnessed and sealed proof of my identity.

Patiently, Louise spent hours with me studying for my national language exam, correcting my faulty grammar and atrocious spelling. With her own brand of Dutch hospitality, she never tired of showing me short-cuts to cycle paths across the city, deciphering the most *in*explicable Mondrian paintings, or introducing me to local traditions, such as how to cook *oliebollen* (traditionally served around New Year's) and *erwtensoep* which became so popular with my family that I have included recipes for both of these in a later chapter.

When I passed my language exam, I was able to count myself among the nearly 20 million people in the world—not a whopping number, compared to English or Chinese—who speak, read and write Dutch. While I may not use my new expertise on a daily basis in the future, learning another language, and an obscure one at that, has enriched my life. I'm sure that I spoke with less than perfect grammar and occasionally, probably more often than I thought, I appeared inept. But it was my experience that the locals appreciated and duly acknowledged any attempt at speaking their language. Thus, my motto was: I would rather speak Dutch and appear foolish than to insist on speaking English and appear arrogant.

The impact of World War II on the Dutch is evident in their conversations and celebrations.

Our fifth day in the Netherlands, while we were still staying in the hotel by the sea and the initial culture shock had not yet dissipated, I insisted on visiting the former hiding place of one of my childhood heroines, Anne Frank. It was a rainy, dreary day in January—typical Dutch winter weather—and we found ourselves waiting in a line 20-people deep along one of the canals in Amsterdam. A city dating from 1275, Amsterdam is known for a series of canals, or *grachten*, that ring the city and help define its many neighborhoods, such as the Jordaan along the *Brouwersgracht,* or the infamous Red-light District on and around *Oudezijds Voorburgwal*, where legal prostitution is offered from street-side windows.

At the very place where the renowned *Diary of Anne Frank* was written and is displayed, we walked through time in the cramped brick structure where the young author had lived in hiding with her family and several family friends for two years during World War II. We peered out through windows in the "attic" on the *Prinsengracht,* where Anne had watched the winter skaters through shaded windows. Reading letters and portions of the diary in Anne's own handwriting had a profound impact on my family. In the midst of a legacy of such historic importance, we were not surprised when we were informed that our fifteen-minute wait had been relatively short; apparently, the line during summer months winds around an entire city block.

About three months later, feeling more adventurous, I traveled to a nearby town north of The Hague called Haarlem. This quaint and ancient town, dating to the 10th century, is known for its 15th century church, nearby tulip fields, and the Frans Hals Museum where work by the famed Dutch painter of the same name is displayed. However, my main interest was none of these; my mission here was a visit inside the former home of Corrie Ten Boom—a member of the Dutch resistance during World War II, who housed and aided countless persecuted individuals. The personal lifesaving contributions of this courageous individual and her tragic experiences during internment in a concentration camp are retold in her now well-known book, *The Hiding Place*.[4] This residence, unlike the Anne Frank House, has relatively few visitors, but the emotional impact of viewing the cramped hidden cavities, where humans were concealed for days in desperation, was just as lasting.

A more regular pastime for us in the Netherlands was strolling along the beach in Scheveningen (fully clothed, I might add, since there were some local traditions we did *not* adopt). On one of our beachcombing expeditions, we stumbled across more than shells in the sand; we observed the top of a green-colored mound just protruding from the top of the sand dunes. Upon closer inspection, we noticed that there was not *one* mound, but several mounds extending to the north of the more populated beachfront.

We inched closer, not wanting to disturb the protected beach grass. To our astonishment, we realized that these strangely shaped objects were remnants of bunkers from World War II—part of the Atlantic Wall the Germans had erected, convinced that the Allies would invade from across The Channel. The sight of Dutch families building sand castles, sunbathing and strolling in front of these bunkers without giving them a second look was somewhat difficult to understand. What these observations made us realize is that the Dutch have always had to live with the remnants of WWII—these lasting reminders are not only a part of Dutch history, but also a part of current life in Holland.

During our visit to the Ardennes, our neighbors spoke at length about their own family experiences during the War. Two uncles were deported to eastern Germany, along with thousands of other Dutch men, to replace the workforce that was now fighting on the eastern and western fronts for the Reich. One uncle escaped by jumping off the train and Tante Mieke's house in Grathem was fortunate to be in the first province liberated by the Allies. In fact, during the fall of 1944, her house provided the local base for Edward Heath, then with the British Artillery and later the Prime Minister of Great Britain.

The British military inhabited the ancestral home and Tante Mieke became one of the many girl couriers aiding the Dutch Resistance and delivering top-secret documents during WWII. Her memories included an interrupted turkey dinner (provided by the kindness of her Majesty of England) on December 16th, when Heath received a phone call and announced that he and his men must immediately depart. This was the onset of the Battle of the Bulge.

Each year on May 4th, Remembrance Day (*Herdenkingsdag*), and on May 5th, the official Day of Liberation from the Nazis (*Bevrijdingsdag*), the Dutch celebrate and remember. We watched the Royal Family lay a wreath in Dam Square in Amsterdam in front of a crowd of thousands that spilled into the side streets—although they were commemorating an event that had taken place nearly sixty years ago—to honor the strength, loyalty and sacrifice of the Dutch people. Later that day, we observed the two minutes of silence at 8:00pm along with the rest of the nation, in honor of the thousands of Dutch who had been deported, brutalized, shot and starved during the Nazi occupation.

It is clear to any expatriate that the events of the Second World War had a lingering and life-altering impact on the Dutch and on their descendants. As expatriate guests in their country, we made a concerted effort to respect and remember the deep imprint that is left on an occupied country during war, and to educate ourselves on the local history. [5-8]

The Dutch are employee-focused, so learn not to complain about slow service and irregular shop hours.

In terms of culture, the same philosophy that encourages a focus on long leisurely holidays for employees also promotes frustration and misunderstandings for temporary residents and tourists; in essence, the employee comes first, not the customer.

While the benefits of this family-friendly philosophy to the employees are on two levels, so are the *in*conveniences to customers. The first priority of the employer is to facilitate flexible hours for employees, so business hours must also remain flexible. This means that the "Open and Closed Hours" stated on the door of any establishment are an estimate at best. We learned to expect stores to open later than posted, which is generally not until noon on Mondays and sometimes Tuesdays, and not to be surprised at window signs stating (of course in Dutch) "Gone for Lunch. Open again at 2."

An important lesson that we eventually learned was to never—and I repeat, never—enter an establishment ten minutes prior to closing, a lesson we often forgot in moments of exhaustion or need. If we happened to lose our senses and dare to race into a store during the final minutes of business, while they were already dangling the keys in their hands, we were rushed, ignored, or asked to leave. After all, we finally began to appreciate their point, their workers needed to get home in time for the family meal!

In addition, few stores were open on Sundays—it was actually illegal for most establishments—so we learned to stock up on necessities, like Bordeaux, Burgundy, and Chardonnay, the day before. Although this "Sunday Law" has been altered for the month of December in honor of *Sinter Klaas*, and also waived for a special *Koopzondag* (Shopping Sunday) from time to time, the available shopping hours during the holidays still pale in comparison to the States. My brother remarked when he was visiting here, "What? I can't do my last minute shopping here at midnight, as I can at the Cambridge Galleria?" I, for one, have found the *lack* of frenzied, fanatical holiday spending sprees a pleasure. In fact, I have concluded that all U.S. stores should severely curtail their holiday hours and post signs in their windows stating "Go home to your family!"

The second priority of the Dutch employer is to enable lengthy vacations. Thus, we discovered that the posted "Open and Closed Hours," besides being estimates, were irrelevant during the summer and long holiday weekends. We were surprised when a few local shops closed for the entire month of July or August, because the owners were spending their annual four-week holiday in Tuscany or southern France. While we applauded this commitment to time-off (the only inconvenience for us being that we had to buy even more wine and cheese in June), we were amazed at the business sense of this decision. After all, these were the two months that The Hague was besieged by busloads of tourists. The owners of these stores could have made enough money during this time to retire early and vacation permanently. However, we soon discovered that many of the locals disappeared during these same months for their own lengthy excursions, so perhaps the owners had better business sense than we realized.

These business closings during the summer were an excellent example of another cornerstone of the cultural philosophy in the Netherlands: make just enough to stay in business and be happy. In fact, there is a Dutch saying that one should not aim to be the tallest ear of corn in the field, for the tallest ear of corn will always be trimmed to equal the height of the rest of the ears in the field. In the Dutch person's mind, one should strive to stay inside the norm.

We assume that this is the reason each small-business owner strives to be as successful as– not *more* successful *than*—his neighbor. There was little turnover at the restaurants we frequented, since there was usually only one seating per night. It did not matter whether our reservations were for 19:00, 20:00, or 21:00, our table remained empty until we arrived, one table per customer per night. Not surprisingly then, many tables remained empty for a large portion of the evening, and customers requesting to be seated were sent away.

If an establishment did not take reservations and was understaffed, tables also remained unfilled. Customers were only seated at those tables that the staff could comfortably (leisurely) handle, even if half the tables remained empty for half the night. We grew accustomed to two-hour lunches, four-hour dinners, thirty-minute droughts between drinks, and eternal waits for the *rekening*—even at the best eating establishments—Irish Pubs not included. The idea, from their perspective, is not to rush.

While my brain understands the logic of the management methods used here, and I have certainly reaped the benefits of the employee-friendly approach, I may forever remain "semi-European." I continued to snatch secretive glances at my watch, to feel guilty about slowly sipping wine over lengthy lunches (even without a meeting to attend), and to gaze in amazement at the unfilled tables and ponder over the inefficiency and lost income for the owners.

I wondered how these small businesses solved their objective function, which is *not* to maximize profit, but to optimize the break-even point, with a sizable constraint on holiday time. I appreciated this pace of life but also realized that none of these businesses would survive in Boston if they closed for a month during tourist season. During our time abroad, our motto was: Eat, drink, and be patient!

The police in the Netherlands are efficient and effective, so learn the local laws.

The police force in the Netherlands is relatively small, but seemingly efficient. I have never seen the Dutch police, for example, eating doughnuts and drinking a *kopje koffie* at the local café. I also have never seen them sitting on the side of a road. (After years of conditioning in the States, every time I saw a stopped car, I thought it was a speed trap and found myself searching for flashing lights.)

The Dutch do not find it necessary to spy and entrap unwitting motorists racing to pick up their children; they have a far less forgiving system: strategically placed cameras along the roadways and at major intersections. While these are now commonplace in the U.S., the Dutch were early adopters of this technology. Unsuspecting motorists should think twice before stomping on the pedal or running a red light. One 'stomp' and *click* their license plate is on film. One month later they will receive a bill in the mail for the speeding ticket with the amount (typically about $50), due date, and bank account clearly marked. Very few *Nederlanders* challenge a ticket. One temporary resident who challenged such a ticket was given the opportunity to see a blow up of his face, up close and personal!

While it is true that those of us who lived in the Netherlands, and traveled the same roads every day, were well aware of the exact location of each and every (well almost) camera in the city, it is nonetheless an effective system. True, traffic slows down before each camera and then speeds up again after passing each camera, but the overall effect is a slower traffic pattern, without the cost of the labor, coffee, and doughnuts for the police on the side of the road. These cameras also free up the *politie* to handle more important business in the city, like searching for all the bikes that are stolen every day.

After having lived in the Netherlands for almost two years, I prided myself on receiving only *one* ticket, and it was not for speeding but for "blocking" an intersection. Of course, my opinion is that I did not deserve this ticket, because I was caught between a green and a red light and was unable to make my turn due to heavy traffic that morning. I quickly paid the ticket, since I had no interest in seeing my morning-face in a blow-up photo that showed every imperfection.

My husband was quite amazed by my lack of speeding tickets, since I drove my children every morning to schools in small towns approximately

20 minutes outside of The Hague—Wassenaar and Voorschoten. He knew that in the past I have been fond of the gas pedal. One disadvantage of the "camera system" is not having the opportunity to negotiate with the Dutch police "face-to-face" and *not* talking, or crying, your way out of a ticket.

Although I did not receive any tickets in the States during the five years before our move, I did receive several "warnings." During a recent speed trap capture prior to our move overseas, as the policeman was making his way back to his squad car, after giving me a warning, my daughter in the back seat blurted out, "Good thing he doesn't know this is your fifth warning, mom!" I held my breath as the cop halted for a moment but, fortunately, he never turned around and I drove off—slowly.

Besides being captured on film, the *politie* in the Netherlands get to know the local citizens quickly by knocking on windows and doors, and making late-night phone calls. Although wearing a seat belt is a law in the States, I have never had a policeman, or policewoman, stop me for *not* wearing one—until now. Since the local *politie* don't need to waste time setting up speed traps, it seems they have that much more time to drive around the city and catch random drivers doing anything out of the ordinary.

After picking up my children one day from school, I found myself stopped at a red light alongside a police car. As I was explaining to my son that he had better behave because the police were watching him, much to my surprise, the policeman rolled down his window and waved to us; it turned out, he *was* watching, not the children, but me. He told me in polite but terse Dutch, "Put your seat belt on—now." My children were proud of themselves, as they should be, because they already had their belts on. The mud was on *mom's* face.

Later that same week, as my husband and I were stopped at a different intersection, I found myself face-to-face with two more policemen, who rapped on our window. I rolled it down and asked (in my best but faltering Dutch), what I could do for them on such a pleasant evening. One of the policemen stated flatly, again, in polite Dutch, "Your left headlamp is out. You should have it replaced immediately—or pay a fine."

I calmly explained that we had an appointment at the local Opel dealer to have the headlamp replaced the following day. He countered, "You should phone the local AWNB (Dutch version of AAA) dealer to have the headlamp replaced immediately."

I inquired if we could wait—since it was now 19:30 and clearly all Opel dealers were closed. His reply was, "That is not a good idea."

I expressed gratitude for his assistance and verified that we were indeed card-carrying AWNB members. We promised to call AWNB as soon as we arrived home—coincidentally, only *one* block away, since before we were stopped, we had been circling our neighborhood looking for a parking place!

The policeman and his partner—with a combined height of well over 13 feet—seemed satisfied and sauntered off. Silently, I thought of informing them that if the Dutch weather was not so damn gray all the time, we wouldn't have to have our headlamps replaced every two months, and doesn't he have better things to do, by the way, like tracking down my stolen bicycle!

Wisely, I held my tongue. Ironically, as they drove off, my husband noted that one of *their* taillights was not operating, and he was full of gusto to inform them of this "man-to-man" (although *our* combined height was decidedly less than 11 feet). But I didn't feel up to the chase, so I informed my "man" that I had used up my quota of Dutch words for one evening.

Another encounter with the Dutch *politie* (we were becoming quite chummy by now) occurred over the telephone (so I have no idea if he was as tall as the rest of the police force) when we received a call at the "hospitable" hour of one o'clock in the morning. It was the weekend of Prince Constantijn's wedding and severe parking restrictions were being enforced in the city. We had received several notices—all in Dutch, but complete with city maps, carefully designating the appropriate streets for parking.

Because of the different events—civil wedding, church wedding, citywide procession, and *koninklijke* barbecue—the "safe" streets varied depending on the day, the hour, and the minute throughout the weekend.

Apparently, said the voice at the other end of the phone line, we had parked on a prohibited street, and our car would be towed if it was not moved before 4:00 this morning.

I have to admit I was never so happy to receive a phone call at 1am as then, even if it was from a cop. Now, this was service! I was only too happy to venture out into the dark, deserted streets to move my car and avoid paying into the royal coffers to retrieve my car. This polite, albeit late-night gesture was vastly different from our experience stateside. During our first five minutes after moving to New Haven, Connecticut, while we were opening a bank account, our car was towed—because rush-hour rules were now in effect on all major streets. I guess everyone in New Haven wears their seat belts, so they have nothing better to do than tow cars!

Here in Holland, the preference is definitely *not* to tow. On many occasions, if there was construction activity in our *buurt*, the *politie* went door-to-door looking for the owners of the parked cars. If no owner could be located, then the last resort was towing. Now, this is what I call a civilized country! I will gladly learn to wear my seat belt, read wedding itineraries, and observe construction signs if it means avoiding speed-traps, towing fees, and the variable-cost of all the doughnuts and coffee-per-policeman-per-hour-per-day.

As a final note on the *politie*, I relate an event that happened to a friend of ours—another expatriate working for Royal Dutch Shell. While sitting in his car waiting for his daughter, he heard a sudden tap-tap-tap on his window. I suppose it seems strange that we always had our windows closed, but remember it rained every month, every week, every day. Our surprised friend rolled down his window. The officer asked, "Do you know that your motor is running?"

In response, the expatriate explained that he was leaving shortly, since he was expecting his daughter in a few minutes, to which the officer replied, "Please turn your motor off, because you are wasting petrol!"

After recovering from his surprise, our friend considered arguing with this request (after all it was cold in the car), but since he didn't know the punishment for wasting petrol at expensive European prices, he obliged and turned off his motor.

Over time, we grew to expect and even enjoy the personal attention of the police force in the Netherlands. Where else could I expect to get a phone call in the middle of the night giving me a chance to move my car before the tow truck arrived?! In the interest of minimizing our chance of ending up in the *gevangenis*, our motto was: Buckle-up for safety, replace headlamps and, by all means, don't waste petrol!

The Dutch believe in freedom of choice and speech—so monitor the airwaves.

Even the former Pilgrims noticed that the Dutch seemed to make merriment, indulge their children, and allow too many freedoms for the taste of the strict separatists. The reputation of the free-spirited Hollanders has endured and continued into the 20th and 21st centuries. A comparison of the legal restrictions, or lack thereof, reveals that some of this reputation is deserved. However, the spirit and soul of this exuberance also lies in the focus on family and the emphasis on tolerance of others—both noble ideals.

Our first week in The Hague, during which we witnessed the celebration of the New Year, was a case in point. While we had been prepared for a celebration, perhaps with a heady hangover, what we observed was a giant block-party that resembled a war-zone for newcomers. The pops from the noisemakers, legal in the Netherlands on this holiday, lasted through the night; the revelry in the streets wafted up through our windows; and the streets resembled the Red Sea—littered with discarded casings. Needless to say, I was alone when I walked our Labrador the next morning on the Scheveningen sand. In fact, not a soul stirred in the entire city until late afternoon on the first of January. Apparently, we had survived baptism by firecrackers for foreigners.

By the same time the following year, we were hosting the New-Year's Eve dinner party ourselves and dancing in the street while hoisting champagne glasses with our new-found neighbors and friends. I think we saw the sunrise. Needless to say, our Labrador had a quick trip to the garden alone the next morning.

The Dutch exuberance and freedom of individual choice was not limited to visible behavior. Some of it was more, shall we say, seductive. Our initial visits to newspaper stands and bookstores provided more surprises, as we realized that our son seemed to enjoy spending lengths of time in specific store aisles. We soon discovered the reason: scintillating skin-magazines that were not standard items on shelves of American establishments—at least not so blatantly. In fact, occasionally, this sordid literature would be up front near the entrance to the Dutch stores, so our senses could not help but be heightened, even if we had not wanted them to be. Thankfully, following the initial excitement of these early glimpses of glossy photos of female body parts, our son's interest waned (or so it seemed) and we also learned what newsstands to avoid.

My Dutch teacher often attempted to explain the local philosophy of tolerance to us in this way: Individuals make their own choices; therefore, they are responsible for the consequences of their actions and decisions. This includes the choice of risky (or risqué) behavior, imbibing of alcohol, taking of drugs, or self-infliction of bodily harm.

This is a tempting concept to buy into, because it removes the responsibility we often feel for our neighbors' behavior and coincides nicely with a society that places emphasis on individualism. However, along with this individualistic notion is the consequence of accepting responsibility for decisions. Holland is not a litigious society. There are no scapegoats, no million-dollar lawsuits over the ill effects of cigarettes, bad needles, or hot coffee. One must accept the consequences of a personal decision: the good, the bad, and the ugly. For example, we never considered suing anyone in the Netherlands over our son's chipped teeth, nor did a friend, whose daughter slashed her foot on a protruding piece of metal in a pool at a local amusement park.

This tolerance also extended to the airwaves. Because I drove the children to school everyday and wanted to practice my Dutch, we became fans of Dutch radio. There was a wide range of music, although much of it was new to us. Between the boy-bands (passionately followed by all their pre-adolescent fans in Holland), I tried to listen to the traffic report and figure out where the *verkeer* was, or when the next trucker's protest would be.

We had already experienced multiple protests while in The Hague, which resulted in road closures and hours of traffic. While we were impatient and could feel our blood pressure rise, most of the Dutch around us took these strikes in stride by kicking a soccer ball and having a picnic. They were more tolerant (naturally) of their fellow trucker citizens than I could ever be.

Thanks to the radio, in addition to learning new Dutch words, my children learned a few new English words—of the four-letter variety. With no, or few, restrictions on what could be stated on the air, the Dutch DJs had a field day and seemed to be in a constant state of competition: Who knew the foulest words and who could say the most in a five-minute interval? As hard as I tried, this assault on my ears every morning was difficult to become accustomed to and it usually resulted in station surfing on my part.

As with radio, television stations were not over-regulated with limits on language or visible images. Thus, the afternoon fare produced a greater variety of slang; the evening fare was definitely more adult; and the nighttime fare was, well, "observed at our own risk." Not a necessarily bad situation, if only we had been prepared for it. Unfortunately, the first time we discovered the dangers of television was when my son had a friend sleep over. The movie they found on a public television station at ten o'clock at night gave new meaning to learning the facts of life through audiovisuals!

Of course, the Dutch would say that the viewing of television should be minimized, and children shouldn't be watching TV after 10:00pm. *Or* they might even say "What's the harm? It's normal." We agreed with the former viewpoint, and learned to monitor late-night television viewing. After that our motto was: It's ten o'clock; do you know what your children are watching?

While my observations of the Dutch lifestyle are not exhaustive, they provide a taste of our experiences in a foreign land—a land that we came to consider home. I know that capturing years of moments into pieces of advice is not possible, so my suggestions are simply "food for thought" for future residents of the Netherlands—the land of long lunches, late store openings, highway cameras, friendly *politie*, and un-rated, uncensored television. Here are my recommendations:

One: Learn the local language.
Two: Discover and appreciate Dutch history.
Three: Eat, drink … and be patient.
Four: Expect irregular shop hours.
Five: Don't leave holiday shopping until the last minute.
Six: Observe the posted speed limit.
Seven: Buckle up for safety and replace headlamps.
Eight: Know what your children are watching.

NOTES

Chapter 5: Learning the Language and Culture

1. Janin, Hunt (1998), *Culture Shock: A Guide to Customs and Etiquette*, Singapore: Times Editions Pte Ltd.
2. van der Horst, Han (2001), *The Low Sky: Understanding the Dutch* (5th Edition), Schiedam: Scriptum Publishers.
3. Vossestein, J. (1997), *Dealing with the Dutch*, Amsterdam: KIT Publishers.
4. Ten Boom, Corrie with John and Elizabeth Sherrill (1971), *The Hiding Place*, New York: Bantam Books.
5. Blom, J.C.H. (1989), *Crisis, Bezetting en Herstel: Tien studies over Nederland 1930–1950*, The Hague: B.V. Universitaire Pers Rotterdam.
6. De Jong, Louis (1990), *The Netherlands and Nazi Germany (Erasmus Lectures 1988)*, Boston: Harvard University Press.
7. Hooker, Mark T. (1999), *The History of Holland*, Westport, CT: Greenwood Press, Inc.
8. Maas, Walter B. (1970), *The Netherlands at War: 1940-1945*, New York: Abelard-Schuman.

Haastige spoed is zelden goed.

Haste makes waste.

Chapter 6

Traveling in the Netherlands

Our observations overseas were not limited to The Hague. As we ventured farther from home, our astonishment and excitement at discovering differences between our two cultures increased.

The preferred means of transportation by the Dutch, the energy-efficient bicycle, is self-evident even to the casual visitor. Although we all owned cycles in the States, our wheels never covered as many miles as in the flat country of the Netherlands.

The Dutch cycle everywhere, so learn to cycle along.

My neighbors did not own a car. This fact, while surprising, did not immediately make an indelible impression. Yes, the father cycled everyday to work, about a 10-minute ride, but this is not far by Dutch standards, and Peter, my husband, also cycled to his office. Yes, the mother next door biked to the shops in the city, but I *walked* everywhere now; she simply got there sooner and besides, she seemed to enjoy it.

As the seasons changed, we began to realize the full impact of not owning a car. Occasionally, Peter would drive to work, typically on days with heavy rainfall. (O.K.... maybe more than occasionally). However, our neighbor, along with seemingly every other worker in the city, continued to ride his bike: in rain, freezing rain, sheeting rain and windswept rain—typical *Nederlandse weer*.

Although I eventually walked or cycled to most destinations, I continued to use my car for the daily excursion to my children's schools and an occasional trip to the grocery store. For me, food shopping with a bike presented a challenge; I always bought too many groceries for my saddlebags and ended up cycling home with eggs balancing on my lap and bags of *groenten* dangling from my handlebars hoping not to bump into another cyclist, since my balance was still that of a *buitenlander*!

I soon discovered how Louise managed to cycle for her food shopping; she packed her saddlebags efficiently and visited the local market almost daily. While daily marketing offered the advantage of fresher produce, this experience was a bit stressful for me. Besides navigating my bicycle through traffic, each trip to the local supermarket required translating food labels (particularly if I couldn't tell what kind of meat I was buying), converting grams to ounces for recipes, bagging all my own groceries (assuming I remembered to bring my own bags), before the long line of locals became mutinous, and remembering to return the cart to get my deposit back. It's a wonder this daily routine didn't give me ulcers!

Louise, on the other hand, was always on her cycle. In fact, I'm convinced she owes her great legs to cycling. Women of all ages in Holland, even those pushing 100, could be seen daily on their three-speeders battling the elements to fetch the daily staples. In my opinion, every modeling agency in the world should set up shop in Holland, at least if they are advertising stockings, mini-skirts, or spike heels.

Our neighbor's three daughters also cycled everywhere. Each morning we passed them cycling to school which was about 15 blocks away through the city streets. During the winter months, this meant riding in the dark (one reason headlights are required on all bikes here), accompanied by their father who would ride with them to school, then turn around and ride the other direction to work. When the children had appointments with a doctor or dentist on the other side of the city, they also rode their bikes there. When the children visited other children, attended birthday parties, or went to the cinema, they rode their bikes. On days they didn't feel well, they rode their bikes. On days they could see their breath in the morning, they rode their bikes. On days it was so windy that you would swear their bikes were flying, they rode their bikes. This was their main source of local transportation. If they traveled outside of The Hague, they traveled by rail.

My neighbors are typical of a Dutch lifestyle. One has only to witness rush hour in The Hague to realize this extraordinary phenomenon. Between the hours of 8 and 9am and 4 and 6pm, bikes appear to outnumber cars; bike lanes complete with separate traffic signals are full to capacity; and bike-parking areas for commuters are overflowing. The one time my husband did not use the bike-parking area (complete with attendants) at the train station, his bike, actually *my* bike that he borrowed that day, was stolen. We were told not to waste our time reporting it and not to expect to see my bicycle again. Bikes—especially nice American mountain bikes—are stolen every day in this country. We were also told not to believe that we could protect ourselves with bike locks, because card-carrying members (or, should I say, clipper-carrying members) of the Dutch bike-street gangs wield the mother-of-all chain cutters.

Despite the high rate of cycle-theft in the city, cycling is still the preferred mode of transportation. While the multitude of bicycles sounds provincial, we did after all live in the center of a major European city and the number of commuters driving cars was not inconsequential. Thus, driving was not a trivial activity. In addition to staying clear of other four-wheeled vehicles, we now had buses (which also had their own lanes), trams (which shared their tracks with our lanes), and finally bicycles. Not a day went by that I did not praise God for delivering me home without incident, whether I was traveling on two wheels, four wheels or two feet.

I've decided that any driver's manual of a car purchased, or rented, in the Netherlands should read: Drivers of automobiles beware, the cyclist is always right. Regardless of clearly posted one-way street signs, lack of visibility, disobeyed bike traffic lights, and bikers traveling three abreast, the driver of an automobile is at fault if sheet metal collides with aluminum—*altijd*! Beware of cyclists leaving (or, should I say, weaving) from Irish Pubs as there is no prohibition of DUI on a bike, at least that we observed.

If an accident does occur, which is not infrequent, it is likely that the collision involves one bike, but multiple bike *riders*. It is common for an entire Dutch family to ride on one bicycle. We frequently witnessed women steering bikes with a baby nestled in a front baby-carrier, two older children riding on rear toddler seats, and other children riding bikes of their own alongside their mother, completing the picture. Had we been on country lanes in the rural farmland of New England, this scene might have been a setting for a Norman Rockwell painting. But this was a common scene on crowded, narrow, city streets in the Netherlands' third largest city.

When faced with two or three such scenes coming towards us on a one-way street, which was barely wide enough for our car let alone the Dutch family on the bike, the word *prayer* came to mind more readily than *provincial*. Thus, our motto was: Bike anytime, anywhere—but drive your car with care!

Family time is a high priority in Holland, so during extended holidays travel... travel... travel.

One ongoing joy of our stay here in Holland was the emphasis on families and focus on children. This was evident immediately. All winter long, for example, we joined the throngs of families (including fathers!) that braved the Noordzee winds to cycle to the sand dunes. During the spring and summer, this was prefaced by packing the supplies; towels, swimsuits (no, we still did not bathe in the nude, or join in the nude volleyball matches), juice boxes, *broodjes*, *kaas*, chips, picnic blanket, buckets and shovels—all neatly packed in our newly-acquired and much-used saddlebags.

How is it that my husband, along with all Dutch husbands, had the time and inclination to accompany us to the beach here? We discovered that the reason is part of the backbone of the Dutch philosophy of culture and the economy: That employees deserve downtime. Time to spend with their families and do other things besides work.

If my husband worked on a weekend in The Hague, albeit a rarity, he was the only person besides one security guard in his 15-story building. He also discovered that he was alone if he worked past six-o'clock in the evening. A typical workday here appeared to be the traditional nine to five with flexible hours accepted for official Dutch holidays and *un*official family business. Our favorite neighborhood dad followed this pattern regularly—or irregularly, depending on the week, the weather and his wishes.

In addition to working less overtime, the Netherlands follows the custom of most European countries with extended holidays. When we began our careers in America, we were thrown a bone of a few hours vacation per year; barely enough time to drive to the local tanning booth, never mind driving to the beach.

We considered ourselves lucky if we were permitted to take weekends off after sweating and toiling for the company for multiple years. In the Netherlands, it is customary for an employee (all employees—from the sanitation engineer to the CEO) to be given eight weeks of holiday, including vacation, national holidays, and sick days per year when they cross the threshold. In fact, bosses can be fined if they work their employees "overtime."

Our house painter explained this to me as the reason for his men leaving the job site early on a Friday, even though it was one of the five sunny days that year in Holland. The men had already worked their 35 hours for the week and it was illegal to demand more. Even before moving here, I was aware that Europeans had longer vacations; however, I never fully appreciated the impact of this additional leisure time on the family.

As a result, Peter was able to take a holiday when the children had *their* holidays which was nearly every month; we became quite efficient at throwing the necessary items in a bag and filling every millimeter of empty space in the car. Of course, crowning the pile and taking up the most space in the rear of our German house-on-wheels was Mickie, our giant black Labrador, who sat perched as a king on a throne with the best view and the most windows to slobber on. We also developed the stamina to drive in our cramped yet cozy 'mobile home' for as long as 15 hours, the necessary time to arrive in the French Alps or the French Riviera. In fact, our son said to us after one such trip, "Mom, remember when we used to complain about the three-hour drive to Nana's house? That will be a piece of cake now!" For an overactive boy who has difficulty sitting through dinner, this was an achievement to be proud of.

Of course, if *we* were traveling during the holidays, so was the rest of the Netherlands. But in typical Dutch style, the country is divided into sections for the national holiday schedule, with each section or school district, if you will, given a slightly different timeframe in an attempt to relieve congestion on the roads. How effective is *that*? Well, yes and no. Since more than one-third of the population lives in the *Randstad*—the area in and around Amsterdam, The Hague, and Utrecht—we still felt as if we were on the road with 5 million Dutch citizens.

Every February, April, and July, the last day of school produces a mass exodus unseen by my husband or me in our lifetime. Oh, sure, on many occasions we had been stalled in the annual backup to the Bourne Bridge over Buzzard's Bay or on the Maine Turnpike after Labor Day weekend, but this was different. There are few major *verkeerswegen* out of Holland heading south—and all cars head south—to the Alps in the winter and the French coast in the summer. This fact creates long lines of patient Dutch drivers, who rarely ever use their horns, all the way through Belgium and Luxembourg, slowly slithering their way to the land of snow or sun.

During one of our trips, after we inched our way out of the Benelux (the region of Holland, Belgium and Luxembourg), we had a few hours reprieve as those vacationers heading towards the Austrian Alps turned west and those dreaming of the slopes near Mont Blanc continued south. We thought we were home free! "This wasn't as bad as we were told," we said confidently, as we exchanged high-fives. The only surprise we had was the frequent sight of men peeing along the roadside, directly along the road, mind you, even though numerous bushes were only steps away, which would have shielded this frequent need to *plassen* from our eyes.

We spent the night in Dijon, where hotels cater to dogs, and Mickie was treated like a king taking a respite from his throne, complete with his own dish, leash and treats. We rose early, grabbed breakfast to go (once an American always an American), and hit the highway "pedal to the metal," thinking we were ahead of schedule.

Then we were faced with our second surprise. The traffic was not as *bad* as we were told; it was *worse*! Antwerp and Brussels were a toboggan run compared to the beltway of Lyon. Nothing had prepared us for this. Soon, we were at a standstill, surrounded by Peugeots, Citroens, Renaults, BMWs and, yes, other Opels, all complete with ski racks.

The digital road signs (French radio was difficult for a novice) informed us of our future: 20 kilometers of crawling, playing countless word games, opening all the food in the car, and praying that the dog would hold his urges. Although, I suppose if men can pee along the roadside, so can dogs. And we were the early birds; we learned that later in the day, the backup reached almost 30 kilometers.

Despite the road rage, the multiple pit-stops for the dog, the endless hours of our children's 'N-Sync' and 'Backstreet Boys' CDs (Peter and I secretly played 'Springsteen' when they napped), and the expensive tolls, our family trip was always a bonding experience. We were thankful when we arrived at the ski chalet safely, although we were overly tired, sticky and surprisingly hungry.

It was our hunger that demanded the most attention, besides the dog's bladder, after a long drive. Thus, on our first night in Vars—a jewel of a French ski resort, claiming to have over 300 days of sun a year—we learned about French retail habits the hard way. We should have known this from living in Holland, but we claimed exhaustion and temporary loss of memory from car fumes. After renting our ski equipment (which cost all of $20/day for a family of four), we decided to shop for our standard supper, a good bottle of French wine at local prices, herb chevre and fresh baguettes. With mouths watering, standing on the stoop of the local food store and ogling the tempting selection, we felt the stiff breeze of the door being closed in our face. We had missed closing time by five seconds; it was 18:00 and *all* the stores were closed.

No problem. We'll just take the children out to eat, we decided. After all, we deserve a treat after our long two-day journey. During the next hour we learned: make reservations or get more doors closed in your face. The second hour we learned: local taverns are not good places for tired children. The third hour we learned: every other family in Vars was also hungry and converged on the same cafes. At 21:00, typical dinner time in France, we found ourselves seated at a quaint establishment that was empty when we arrived, but standing-room-only when we left. We literally inhaled the fresh bread, chevre salad, and bottle of Bordeaux. Even the children were adventurous with their tastes, didn't complain, and practiced their novice French. Not bad for a fatigued family that had been in a confined space for far too long!

The good news about Vars is that they were telling the truth about the sun and we enjoyed days of skiing *sans* hats, goggles or coats. (Except for the one day when we were surprised with a meter of snow in a squall that literally shut the tiny Alpine village down.) Of course, it's helpful if you speak French. Thus, we relied on my husband's modest knowledge of the local tongue, although he pleaded the Fifth Amendment in having misread the posted "Closing Hours" in the cafe window. Hence, my daughter's motivation to study French—no more fear of starvation during vacation. Not surprisingly, our trip motto became: Always pack enough food for 15 hours on the road and dinner the first night.

The Dutch care about the environment—
so learn to travel by rail.

Of course, we have all heard about the high price of gasoline in Europe and have considered ourselves fortunate these many years to be blessed with affordable and available fuel for our SUVs on American soil (except for that time in the late 1970s when I could only buy gas on Tuesdays and Thursdays because I had an odd-numbered license plate). The Europeans, however, don't want, or deserve, our pity for higher prices at the pumps. They are proud that they are required to pay this tax, or ecological penalty, for fuel. Their logic is that a higher price for the gasoline, or petrol, will deter drivers from 1) buying a car—recall that my neighbors and many other *Nederlanders* did not own a car; 2) buying a *large* car—our mini Opel station wagon was the largest car on our street; and 3) *driving* a car—remember that biking 10 miles is to a *Nederlander* as walking 10 minutes is to an American.

Once the initial shock of paying over 100 Gulden (the local currency before the Euro came into existence, and about $50 at the time) to fill up our tank had passed, we also adopted the attitude of "to drive is demonic, to cycle is divine." My husband shed pounds and problems as he cycled to and from work every day. I attempted, but never really had any hope, to develop those gorgeous Dutch legs of my neighbors as I cycled to the nearest grocery store at least three times a week, as our saddlebags were small, and the mini-refrigerators were energy efficient. Our children enjoyed the weekend bike trips to the nearby beach in Scheveningen, although they could never understand why they were the only ones in The Hague wearing helmets. Apparently, ecology is a higher priority than safety regulations. (After all, recall that the individual has the right to harm himself.)

Besides hailing the benefits of cycling, the entire public transportation system in the Netherlands and across Europe deserves more than an honorable mention, it deserves to be emulated. (Amtrak, are you listening?) The high-speed train from The Hague to Paris, via Antwerp and Brussels is convenient, comfortable, and most of all fast! In just three-and-one-half hours, my husband and I were in Gare de Nord, Paris, ready to drink in the air, the art and the ambience of our favorite European city. OK, now our *second* favorite city, after The Hague.

Of course, the smaller cities of Antwerp and Brussels were worthy of trips in themselves and, if you are fond of hefty women "playing" with angels, you won't be disappointed in the Rubens here. An even more enticing and romantic city in Belgium, although more difficult to arrive at by train, is Bruges or *Brugge* (pronounced with a soft "g" by the French, and with a guttural "g" by the Dutch). The original home to lace and chocolate when it was once a seaport, this picturesque village has remained in the Renaissance, ever since the shifting of the ocean shoreline removed its elite trading status. Besides the time-capsule aspect of this small Flemish town, the best things I found here were the beer and mussels, with the more garlic, the better.

Resisting our desire to drive and sustaining our rally to rail, we turned our attention eastward and decided to visit Germany. It is not as romantic as France, and not as quaint as Belgium, we found, but equally interesting. I had studied in Heidelberg and toured Germany 20 years ago and, as my husband says, my memory is "good, but short." I chose a weekend trip to Cologne or *Köln* to experience the annual *Weihnacht Markt,* where I heard one could find hand-crafted items for reasonable prices and be warmed internally by glasses of Glühwein at the same time. My kind of shopping experience!

The market did not disappoint, even my husband, the non-shopper, found things to purchase. Unfortunately, because of an incident at our hotel, our personal memories of Cologne are not as pleasant as the "O Tannenbaum" music playing at the *Markt*.

Although I had made our reservations several weeks in advance, to our dismay the hotel had lost any record of the reservation. As a result, we were given two rooms on separate floors in different wings of the hotel, dividing our family in half. Being the customer, I wanted to discuss the service of the hotel with the woman behind the front desk. However, I foolishly forgot that "service" is not a top priority in most German hotels, and the clerk seemed to be telling me that I should be happy we were not sleeping on the street.

At that point, I had a deranged idea, believing that eight years of studying the German language would not fail me. I conjured up the phrases in my mind, convinced myself that I could communicate, and went for it. Bad idea. The reaction from the hotel clerk was not what I had expected; apparently, Dutch was streaming from my mouth and she was insulted. If there is one thing I have learned, it is never to speak Dutch in Germany and never to speak German in Holland!

Turning our attention later to the southern tip of the Netherlands, where you can practically see Belgium if you look westward and see Germany if you look eastward, we decided to treat my parents who were visiting from New York to a weekend retreat in the city of Maastricht. My mom, for whom the phrase "fear of flying" is an understatement, was still recovering from her flight, and was, on top of it, a bit nervous about doing the entire trip by rail. I calmly reassured her that we had traveled by train several times already and that I knew how to read the signs. I could even use my new-found knowledge of Dutch to ask questions if the unlikely need arose. What could go wrong?

We boarded the train in The Hague, with anticipation of our visit to the historic city of Maastricht, the site of medieval conflicts (part of the original Roman wall encircling the city still remains) and more recently, the first Dutch city liberated during World War II. We settled into our seats, equipped with water bottles, snacks and reading material.

After we had traveled approximately half the distance to our destination, we heard abrupt and rapid Dutch over the public announcement system. So rapid, that I had difficulty understanding the message. The passengers around us appeared concerned and began reaching for their bags and preparing to disembark the (still moving) train. What had I missed? My parents began to bombard me with questions. What had the announcer said? Why couldn't I understand him? Why had I said I could speak the language? What if we missed our stop?

Although I tried my best to act composed, the aroused chatter and shuffling of baggage by those around me started to make me nervous. What could be happening? Our transfer station was not for another hour.

Finally, I decided to stop acting like a male who hates to ask for help and ask a stranger what was happening? I eyed what appeared to be a kind, well-dressed, older Dutch woman across the aisle, who I thought would be able to make out my mangling of her language. "What was the announcement about?" I asked with trepidation. (I had been studying Dutch for only three months at this point, and this was, unfortunately, not one of the practiced phrases.)

Apparently, there were structural problems with the rail lines ahead, thus causing a disruption in the service. The plan was to have everyone disembark, board multiple buses, and travel by bus to the next rail station that had a connection to Maastricht. No problem. Although my parents began to panic, I calmed them down; we packed up our snacks and reading material and prepared to follow the other passengers. The plan was logical, and I had more faith than my mother, who was used to New York trains, that the Dutch were organized enough to pull it off.

We were not disappointed. Even my mother was impressed. The buses were waiting for us at the next train station and, with the exception of my father nearly disembarking too early, and all of us nearly boarding a bus to Arnhem, we survived the bus trip and the final segment of the train ride to Maastricht.

Thank goodness our hotel was directly opposite the train station and a short walk to the old city center. There were no more planes, trains, buses or automobiles the rest of the weekend. I continue to stress that the most important aspect of a hotel is location, location, location. As we continued to journey by train, we learned to expect the unexpected, to keep practicing our Dutch, and to appreciate the accessibility of nearby towns and villages without having to navigate the *verkeerswegen.* Our overriding motto was always the same, even for the men in my family: Don't be afraid to ask for assistance, in Dutch, English or whatever language you know.

Our most memorable trip by train was a visit to Nijmegen—one of the oldest cities in the Netherlands.

Nijmegen lies southeast of The Haguc on the Waal river, just south of thc Lower Rhine. Because of its strategic location, its rich history has revolved around a cycle of battle, peace and prosperity. During the first century, the Romans settled here due to the strategic location on the river and called the area *Noviomagus* or 'new market.' However, it wasn't until 1230 that Nijmegen finally became a city in its own right.[1, 2]

Nijmegen has the dubious distinction of being the last major town before the bridge across the Rhine to Arnhem. In September of 1944, U.S. and British Airborne forces landed in the vicinity of Nijmegen and Vegel in preparation for the allied assault called "Operation Market Garden." This battle for the bridge across the Rhine was considered strategic in crossing into northern Holland and marching west to liberate The Hague and Amsterdam. The battle for this bridge was depicted in the book and subsequent movie, *A Bridge too Far.*[3]

However, it was not until the spring of 1945 that the Allies finally freed the eastern towns of Holland and began marching west over the Ijssel river. Between the failed attack at Arnhem and the eventual liberation of

Amsterdam, the Dutch people survived one of their worst winters in history. During the *hongerwinter* of 1944, thousands of Dutch died from mass starvation; Dutch men between the ages of 16 and 40 were rounded up and transported east to labor camps during German raids (*Razzia*); and Anne Frank was discovered and captured in her hideaway in Amsterdam. By the time Arnhem was freed, approximately seven months after the fatal attempt to capture the bridge by paratroopers, the city was devastated. For more information on these fateful and final months of WWII, see Heaps, 1976;[4] or Burgett, 1999.[5]

Nijmegen's historic buildings and *straten* were also destroyed, because of its proximity to the war front. The city center and many of the historical sections needed to be reconstructed, including the *benedenstad* and the shopping and residential districts. When Marie Louise and I visited her family home, then being renovated by her sister, and strolled along the *Waalkade*, the restored walk along the Waal, she pointed to the bridge and the few narrow homes that survived along the river. Reminiscing about her younger days, she retold war stories handed down from her parents and Tante Mieke. Her primary school was brand new when she attended it because the former school had been destroyed during the war—resulting in many fatalities—and her high school days were spent exploring the deserted area near the river, where bombed-out houses remained in a state of disrepair until sufficient funds were available to restore them.

We visited the central market square, the site of the weekly *Grote Markt* surrounded by curved archways and ancient (by U.S. standards) stately buildings that reflect the historical stature of Holland as a trading power. The *Waag*, or the weigh house, a common site in many Dutch cities, was "updated" in the seventeenth century, and again more recently. Today it contains a cozy café and restaurant. We enjoyed a *kopje koffie* at the outdoor café in the square, since the sun was shining—a rare occasion even in southern Holland. Also in the city center is St. Stephen's church, dating from medieval times, with a rebuilt tower and organ, both damaged during the fall of 1944. The organ was actually built in 1776 by Ludwig Konig from Köln and has undergone multiple repairs in the past few centuries.[6]

A tour of Louise's ancestral home just a few steps from the *Waalkade* was nearly as impressive as the city itself, with its towering ceilings, ornate woodwork, and center staircase. The architecture in the Netherlands has never ceased to impress us with its gabled facades and attention to detail. In every town we visited, regardless of size, we spent days craning our necks looking at the varied rooflines, windows, and winches of old Dutch homes. We now understand why guidebooks recommend lining up appointments with your back specialists when you return home. It is no accident that one of the hottest selling pieces of Delftware, the blue and white ceramics for which Holland is known, is the line of small-scaled Dutch buildings: all narrow and four stories tall, each one representing a different style of gable.

That evening in Nijmegen, we cooked a *typisch Nederlandse* meal together; although the definition of a "typical Dutch meal" may depend on the season and geographic region of the country. Marie Louise is an outstanding cook, so we were treated to a full display of authentic Dutch cooking. The appetizer was an assortment of fish, including herring and *gerookte paling* (smoked eel), which was delicious, once we found our nerve to try it. The main meal was a thick beef stew and *zuurkoolpastei* (sauerkraut pie) that was so delectable that I have included the recipe in the next chapter.

Louise has been generous in helping me navigate the local *vismarkt* and *kaaswinkel*, as well as in sharing her family recipes. I can't imagine spending time in Holland without experimenting in the kitchen with the local *groenten*, so I decided that it was time I learn how to cook. I mean *really* learn how to cook. Thus my new motto was: Experiment and take tips from a local cook.

In reminiscing about our travels, I have tried to share many of our warm memories of the Dutch people and food—even the eel. While we visited more places than I have included here, the small Dutch villages full of tradition and not mentioned in any guidebook were often the most revealing. When traveling in and around the Netherlands, I suggest the following:

One:	Cycle anywhere—but drive with care.
Two:	Take advantage of the holidays.
Three:	Be patient in traffic.
Four:	Travel by rail.
Five:	Always pack enough food for 15 hours.
Six:	Ask for assistance.
Seven:	Look up—observe the rooflines.
Eight:	Experiment with local foods.

NOTES

Chapter 6: Traveling in the Netherlands

1. *www.gonijmegen.nl/uk/history.html*
2. *www.missgien.net/nijmegenstories/archives*
3. Ryan, Cornelius (1974), *A Bridge Too Far*, New York: Simon and Schuster.
4. Heaps, Leo (1976), *The Evaders*, New York: William Morrow and Company, Inc.
5. Burgett, Donald R. (1999), *The Road to Arnhem*, Novato, CA: Presidio Press, Inc.
6. *www.orgelland.nl/orgels/nijmegen/history.htm*

Wie niet waagt, wie niet wint.

Nothing ventured, nothing gained.

Chapter 7

Creating a Cook

It is hard to believe, but I never learned how to cook. I don't mean gourmet meals, but simple standard fare. It is not my mother's fault. She taught me how to bake and I can bake pies and Christmas cookies with confidence. In fact, one of the greatest compliments I ever received was early on in my baking career: "It just isn't fair that a teenager can bake such a perfect pecan pie!" But *baking* is not the same as *cooking*.

When my husband and I entertained, the standard assortment of monthly dinner parties and the annual holiday party, he cooked. Yes, the Gods smiled on me and provided me with a husband who is a natural in the kitchen. You know the type: never needs a recipe, never measures anything, tries new ingredients like I try new shampoo, and everything tastes delicious and looks like it belongs on the cover of a cookbook. Clearly, this is not me. Thus we have always had an arrangement: he cooked and I washed dishes. And all was right with the world.

My lack of culinary expertise was not a secret. I have always openly admitted that I was inept in the kitchen. The standard joke in my family was that I specialized in Cajun cooking, because everything I prepared was blackened—fish, meat, tacos, pizza ...and even toast.

My colleagues used to tease me that my children *must* be tired of pasta by now! (Hey, at least I could boil water.) How was it that we were not all as round as tubes of macaroni? I boldly provided a simple explanation. For the previous six years, while my husband and I had lived apart, the children and I had eaten cereal and milk every night for dinner. At this point, my stunned colleagues asked why my children, who were toddlers at the time, never complained about the lack of variety in their diet. I calmly replied that they had a great amount of variety—they could choose among Cheerios, Corn Flakes, Rice Krispies or oatmeal. It made perfect sense to me. What was the problem? After all, I had provided wholesome meals complete with ten essential vitamins and minerals!

So what changed? Why do I now enjoy cooking and serving my children more than Cheerios? The change is simple—time.

To enjoy and appreciate the creativity of cooking, make time.

I never seemed to have the time to cook, since meals were crammed between faculty meetings, after-school sports, homework hour, and bedtime rituals, as they were for most families that I knew. In Holland without the added pressure of a full-time job I had time to plan, purchase and prepare. I had time to shop, chop, dice, slice and even sauté.

Living in a European city, I found the time spent shopping for ingredients the most enjoyable. Within easy walking distance were a variety of local specialty shops: *kaaswinkels, slagerijen, Italiaanse winkels, bakkerijen,* and *wijn winkels*. A *groentemarkt* just a few blocks from our house sold 15 different kinds of mushrooms that I had never heard of, let alone used in my kitchen.

Not only did I purchase the mushrooms, but I also enjoyed finding uses for each type. Not bad for a woman who rarely used the stove. From

Cheerios to chanterelles! This shows that there is hope for all of us who insist on saying, "I can't cook."

While my husband prefers Italian food, and he can concoct anything (his creations continue to be superior) with *boter*, *basilicum*, *knoflook*, and pecorino *kaas*, we also experimented with the local fare. Fish is extremely popular in the Netherlands, because the fresh product is easy to get. *Schol*, *tarbot*, and *haring* seem to be the local favorites. Each summer brings the celebration of the herring catch. A common sight was throngs of people placing raw herring topped with chopped onions in hotdog buns and crunching their way down to the tail, as they strolled along the boardwalk in Scheveningen.

Having lived for several years in the state of Maine, we were more accustomed to watching the lobstermen fill their traps with the raw, slimy fish in hopes of a good day's catch. Thus, this was an odd sight for us New Englanders. On recent visits to Maine, I have tried to convince the lobstermen that if they fed their herring to the Dutch, instead of the lobsters, they could make more money, but they don't believe me.

While fish is a local staple in the kitchen, if one dines out in The Hague (or orders in), Indonesian food tops the list. Apparently, this tradition dates back to the Dutch dynasty when the Netherlands governed Indonesia and installed successful trade routes. The two countries have continued their import/export traffic and Indonesian restaurants are plentiful, ranging in price from corner take-out stands to full-fledged, five-star places of fine dining.

The most popular Indonesian dish is *nassi goreng* and when entertaining individuals from out-of-town, the meal of preference is *rijsttafel*; an Indonesian buffet composed of a variety of rice and meat dishes spiced with *kerrie* and *komijn*. In fact, the eastern influence has made these two spices far more common in the Netherlands than in the States, and they are used as flavor in almost everything. *Kumijn* soon had a permanent place in my Dutch spice cabinet.

Another staple of the Dutch diet is ham and eggs, but not necessarily together. Ham is often used as a substitute for other meats and we were surprised to find ham in many dishes where we expected ground beef (e.g., lasagna). Eggs accompany most dishes, including *nassi goreng*, in which they were delivered sunny-side-up "staring at you" from atop the rice. While my son never got used to this, as an egg-lover, I was in heaven.

As long as I can remember, I have eaten an egg a day—every day. (Yes, I also ate eggs in addition to Cheerios.) In fact, my favorite noontime meal in The Hague was an *uitsmijter*, an open-faced sandwich with two slices of ham and two fried eggs (tomatoes optional). The best thing about the *uitsmijter* was that I could order it after 10:00am without the waiter responding, "I'm sorry, Maam, but we are no longer serving breakfast. (The *real* story behind my earlier complaint at the Cologne hotel was that they had refused to serve me eggs at 9:55am since breakfast ended at 10:00am—and this was more than I could take.)

Besides eggs, the Dutch are fond of a different yellow and white substance—cheese—which they produce in great quantities here. This was another benefit of living in Holland for me, since cheese also topped my list of favorites, second only to eggs and Cheerios in my diet. After all, you don't have to cook cheese. Between the *Leerdammer, Maaslander, Komijnekaas, Geitenkaas, Limburger, Stolwijker,* and *Gouda*, I fell hook, line and sinker.

We ate cheese morning, noon and night, and even our Labrador seemed to appreciate the new variety in flavor and texture. Actually, he recognized the change in odor the most, and preferred the soft smelly cheeses. In fact, the Dutch have a saying that to truly appreciate a new culture, you must experience the culture *in geuren en kleuren*—in odors and colors, meaning "in detail."

Here, I share a sample of recipes that are native to the Netherlands. A few books exist in English on local food and where to find it[1, 2] and a few good recipes can be found in more comprehensive books on Dutch cooking.[3-5] However, I learned to navigate the Dutch markets through trial and error and owe any cooking insights and most of the recipes I have acquired to my Dutch neighbor and close friend, Marie Louise Grooten, a culinary wizard. I have included recommendations, where possible, which may make the recipes more suitable for modern tastes.

Erwtensoep (pea soup)

This is traditional Dutch soup that is good for cold rainy days—traditional Dutch weather.

500 gm split peas (*spliterwten*)
2½ liters water
200 gm bacon or ham (*spek*)
1 large leek (*prei*)
1 small celery root (*knolselderij*)
1 large potato (*aardappel*)
3 sprigs of parsley (*peterselie*)
1 large smoked sausage (*rookworst*)
salt and pepper (*zout en peper*)

Rinse the split peas, then soak in the water for about one hour. Cook the peas in the same water over a low fire. Slice and add to the split peas the following ingredients: bacon or ham, leek, celery root, potato, and celery sprigs (not stalks). Allow soup to cook for another ½ hour until the peas are tender and the soup is beginning to thicken. Add *rookworst* and cook for another 20 minutes over a low fire. (Be sure *not* to boil the soup after adding the rookworst.) Add more water if the soup becomes too thick. Remove the rookworst and slice into pieces. Add the rookworst pieces back to the soup and stir to desired consistency. Season with salt and pepper to taste. Serve with brown bread.

Notes:
This is a hearty soup from Marie Louise. When I used the spek, I cooked it first in a separate pan, then drained the grease before adding to the soup. The knolselderij may be difficult to find, so I often substituted a turnip and found that carrots or chickpeas were a nice addition.

Oudhollandse Oliebollen (Dutch donuts or fritters)

This is a traditional Dutch dessert during the holidays.

500 gm flour (*bloem*)
20 gm yeast (*gist*)
¼ liter milk (*melk*)
1 egg (*ei*)
3 tbsp sugar (*suiker*)
¼ liter dark beer (*bruin bier*)
1 tsp salt (*zout*)
powder sugar (*poedersuiker*)
100 gm raisins (*rozijnen*)
50 gm currants (*krenten*)
50 gm candied orange peel (*oranjesnippers*)
1 diced apple (*gesnipperde appel*)

Place the flour in a mixing bowl. Add the yeast. Add one tablespoon of sugar and one tablespoon of milk. Stir/knead into dough, then cover the bowl with a towel and set aside. After 15 minutes add the remaining sugar and milk, along with the salt, beer, and egg. Stir then add the raisins, currants, chopped orange peel, and diced apple. Mix well then set the dough aside to rise for one hour. Drop by tablespoonfuls into hot oil, which has been preheated on the stovetop. When the oliebollen are brown, remove them, drain on paper towels, and roll in powdered sugar.

Notes:
These are traditionally served on New Year's Eve. The first eight ingredients form the basic recipe and the remaining ingredients are optional. Store in the refrigerator if serving the next day, then reheat and re-roll in sugar.

Andijviestamp (endive or chicory mash)

This is such a common Dutch staple, that it is sold as a "pre-made" dish in the cooler case at the local grocery store. However, the homemade version below is much tastier!

1 large chicory or endive (*andijvie*)
500 gm potatoes (*aardappels*)
100 gm butter (*boter*)
125 ml hot milk (*hete melk*)
salt (*zout*)
pepper (*peper*)
nutmeg (*nootmuskaat*)
1 tsp white vinegar (*wittewijnazijn*)
1 tsp soy sauce (*ketjap*)

Boil the potatoes until soft. Drain and mash potatoes. Add butter and hot milk. Season with salt, pepper and nutmeg to taste. Mash again. Chop the chicory into small pieces (if not already done). Add the chicory to the mashed potatoes, and stir in the white vinegar and soy sauce. Serve with pickled onions or small dill pickles.

Notes:
This is a simple way to spice up mashed potatoes and is an excellent side dish for lamb, beef, pork or ham. A variation of this dish is called "stamppot" and includes other vegetables (mainly carrots), besides the chicory.

Rode Kool (red cabbage)

This is an easy dish to make and makes a nice side dish for a winter luncheon or evening meal.

1 small red cabbage (*rode kool*)
50 gm butter *(boter)*
3 cloves *(kruidnagel)*
2 apples (*appels*)
1 tbs. sugar *(zuiker)*
vinegar to taste (*azijn*)
salt (*zout*)

Remove any leaves of the cabbage that are damaged or wilted. Rinse and slice or shred the cabbage, then dispose of the core of the cabbage. Melt half the butter in a skillet, then add the red cabbage, cloves and sliced apples to the butter. Add one cup of water to the vegetables, cover the skillet, then simmer between 30 and 40 minutes. Add the remaining butter, the sugar, the vinegar and salt. Cook for 5 more minutes, then serve.

Zuurkoolpastei (sauerkraut pie)

This is a common Dutch meal or side dish during the winter months. The taste of the sauerkraut is subdued in this flavorful "quiche" and this is one of my favorite dishes.

500 gm sauerkraut (*zuurkool*)
100 gm bacon (*ontbijtspek*)
5 tsp vegetable oil (*slaolie*)
1 large onion (*ui*)
2 tsps flour (*bloem*)
1 egg (*ei*)
1/8 liter sour cream (*zure room*)
1 pie crust
salt *(zout)*
pepper *(peper)*

Cook the bacon until crispy, then break into pieces. Cut the sauerkraut fine (if not already done) and chop the large onion. Beat the egg, then mix with the sour cream. Mix in a separate bowl the sauerkraut, the bacon pieces, the chopped onion, the vegetable oil and the flour. Pour over the egg/cream mixture and blend until uniform. Add salt and pepper to taste.

Place the pre-made pie crust in a pie dish. Fill pie crust with the sauerkraut mixture and use any leftover dough to place in strips on top of the mixture. Bake for 60-75 minutes in the oven at 400° F (205 C).

Notes:
Marie Louise served this as a side dish to a heavy meat stew. I found that the pie was done after 45 minutes and that 6 ounces of bacon added sufficient flavor. If using sauerkraut that is pre-cut, drain before adding.

Rijstpudding (rice pudding)

This is a traditional Dutch dessert—perfect for a cold winter afternoon or evening.

1cup rice (*rijst*)
2½ cups milk (*melk*)
pinch of salt (*zout*)
4 tbsp sugar (*suiker*)
1 tsp vanilla (*vanilla*)
2 eggs (*eieren*)
Grated rind of ½ lemon (*citroen*)
1/3 cup raisins (*rozijnen*)
1 tbsp butter (*boter*)

Bring the rice to a boil in the milk with the salt, sugar and vanilla. Simmer till tender for about 40 minutes. Stir frequently. Remove this mixture from the stove and stir in two beaten eggs, lemon rind and raisins. Grease a baking dish with the butter. Pour in the rice mixture. Bake the pudding in a moderate oven (325°F/165°C) for about 30 minutes, until the pudding is set.

Notes:
This recipe is from The Art of Dutch Cooking by C. Countess van Limburg Stirum.[3] *However, her recipe calls for lining the baking dish with breadcrumbs and serving with strawberry or raspberry sauce. I prefer this dish without the breadcrumbs and served with a sprinkle of cinnamon and nutmeg with a topping of whipped cream for added sweetness. The raisins are optional, and using only ½ cup rice will make a softer pudding.*

Notes

Chapter 7: Creating a Cook

1. American Women's Club of Amsterdam (1995), *Holland Days: A Collection of American and Other International Recipes adapted for the Dutch Kitchen*, Delft: Eburon Publishers.
2. Koene, Ada Henne (2000), *Food Shoppers' Guide to Holland*, 3rd edition, Delft: Eburon Publishers.
3. Halverhout, Heleen A.M. (1972), *Dutch Cooking,* Amsterdam: De Driehoek Publishers.
4. Keatinge, Hilary and Anneke Peters (1995), *The Flavour of Holland*, Haarlem: Schuyt & Co., Uitgevers BV.
5. van Limburg Stirum, C. Countess (2001), *The Art of Dutch Cooking*, New York: Hippocrene Books.

Hij waagt zich in het hol van de leeuw.

He takes huge risks.

Chapter 8

Educating a Dynamo

When we realized we would be moving to The Hague instead of Paris, I quickly began researching the educational alternatives. If we wanted an English-speaking environment, we had few choices: a British School in the nearby farming community of Voorschoten, an American School in the upscale suburb of Wassenaar, or an International School on the edge of the city. If we wanted a Dutch-speaking environment, we had a choice of the local public school, or multiple private and religious schools in the vicinity of The Hague. The Dutch school selection appeared complicated for our daughter Katrina (already 11), but appeared realistic for our younger son Peter (then 9), so we weighed the options.

The Dutch pride themselves on a strong education system.

The Dutch literacy rate has been estimated as high as 99%, compared to slightly less in the United States and Canada. School is mandatory between ages 5 and 16. Children attend elementary or "primary" school first, where most are introduced formally to English as a second language during their final year. Thus, Dutch children begin learning English at the age of 11 or 12.

Most children, however, are introduced to American slang at a much younger age through popular rock songs, television reruns of old sitcoms, and Hollywood movies. In fact, we were told that Hollywood is to blame for the fact that the first English word Dutch children learn is of the four-letter variety. (I maintain it is the over-zealous and unregulated Dutch DJs who are to blame.)

Between primary and "secondary" schools, children are tested and sent to vocational, general, or pre-university secondary schools. Education at junior general schools (MAVO) lasts four years, while education at senior general secondary schools (HAVO) lasts five years. A pre-university school (VWO) lasts six years, and includes specific courses in preparation for advanced studies at a university. Many students at general schools do not continue onto a university, although it is still an option. The vocational schools (VBO) educate the skilled laborers of the country, including mechanics, nurses and workers in the service industry.

It is well known that the government subsidizes education in Holland. However, over one-half of the country's primary and secondary schools are affiliated with a church, and typically charge tuition, although a nominal amount compared to private schools in the States. While universities are partially funded for residents, admission to a university, particularly the one of your choice, is highly competitive due to limited space. Thus, if Dutch residents are bright and have a degree from a solid pre-university school, they have a good chance at receiving an education at a very low cost, relative to the cost of university in the States.

The Netherlands has a strong public university system.

The most well-known of the Dutch universities are among the oldest in Europe. For example, the University of Leiden was formed in 1575 and was well-established by the time the separatist Puritans resided in Leiden before departing for America in 1620. Although Dutch residents may apply to any university, many of the universities have become recognized in specific fields, resulting in enhanced competition for admission. The University of Leiden is known for medical and life sciences, while Rotterdam is known for economics and business.

While we did not need to worry about university applications, we did need to decide on primary and secondary schools for our children. This decision, which was largely driven by availability of open spots, was simpler in regards to our daughter and we ultimately decided on an English-speaking environment for her. However, we had to learn a new dialect after she enrolled in The British School and we were introduced to her favorite expressions: "Cheerio"—*not* meaning her favorite childhood dinner—and "Bloody Hell, Mum"—obviously showing her adolescent frustration and new-found "culture."

For our son, the decision was more difficult and we settled on the nearby American School, since it miraculously had an opening in his grade level. Retrospectively, we wish we had given the local Dutch school more consideration. Besides the likelihood that Peter would have learned Dutch more rapidly, our difficulties with a rigid, inflexible, and privileged private school might have been avoided. While the students at The American School were not homogeneous, since they represented nearly all fifty states and a diverse set of global experiences, their learning styles were assumed to be universal, rather than unique.

I knew that our son was different when I looked out my kitchen window and saw him seated atop our 40-foot pine tree. As I yelled to him to climb down "immediately," I waited at the bottom of the tree with shaking knees and outstretched arms. I quickly realized that he needed no help in scaling the tree and was absolutely fearless; an expert tree climber at the tender age of two. Of course he was ignorant of the consequences if he missed a branch!

This was just the beginning. As he developed physically, we continued to observe our son preferring to play *on top* of structures, rather than *in* or *around* them. Shortly after the tree incident, during a visit to my mother-in-law's, we decided to let the children get some fresh air at a nearby playground. After a series of successful adventures on the swings, seesaws and monkey bars, we felt confident enough to give him a bit of running room. Not a good idea. Moments that seemed like microseconds after we saw him walking *towards* the playhouse, what we thought was a "safe" piece of equipment , we found him walking *on* the peak of the roof, like an acrobat balancing on a tightrope.

We asked ourselves, Why does our toddler climb trees? Why does he scale the biggest and sharpest rocks? Why does he want to ski the expert slopes with my husband; straight down the mountain!? Why does he snorkel the reefs with no fear? Why does he thrive on activities that would daunt most children? Our neighbors in Maine used to say, "That is a boy who is going places. We don't know where he is going, but he is definitely going places!"

I reduced my teaching load to spend more time with him, but his temperament remained inexplicable. Visits to the pediatrician were both comforting and frustrating. I recall a typical conversation with my son's doctor that resembled the following:

Me: *Doctor, I believe that my son is overactive.*

Doctor: *Why do you believe this?*

Me: *Well, he prefers running to walking. I'm always chasing him. He will not sit in his stroller and constantly tries to climb out of his car seat.*

Doctor: *He sounds like a typical toddler to me. This is why this phase of a child's life is called "the terrible twos."*

Me: *But, he is three now!*

Doctor: *In many children, this phase lasts longer.*

One year later, another visit to the same pediatrician produced the following conversation:

Me: *Doctor, I still think that my son is more active than other children.*
Doctor: *Why?*
Me: *Well, is it normal to make four trips to the emergency room during one year?*
Doctor: *For what reasons?*
Me: *Two possible concussions—from running and falling in the house and two possible broken hands—from a slammed car door and a house window.*
Doctor: *These are common childhood accidents... he sounds "all boy" to me.*

What was a young mother to do? The defensive meetings with his preschool teachers and the awkward glances from the other mothers (all with timid, obedient, daughters) continued. Just prior to leaving Maine, one final incident occurred that remains memorable. Our son had developed an affinity for the TV character McGyver: a swashbuckling inventive problem-solver. The TV program was harmless and non-violent by modern standards, so we enjoyed watching it with the children. One day, while I was on the phone, I realized the house was far too quiet. Usually, I can't speak for more than two seconds without hearing a child demanding my attention. In a panic, I raced around the house looking for my son. I found him on the second floor, standing next to an open window in the bathroom tying a piece of rope to the handle.

Me: *Stop! What are you doing?*
Son: *(Looking at me with wide innocent eyes, as he is putting the finishing touches on his square knot.) Oh, hi mom...look, I am just like McGyver!*

He explained to me with a rush of excitement how he was going to propel himself out the window down the side of the house—just like McGyver had done the day before. At the time our son was four. Needless to say, thereafter we kept all ropes under lock and key.

Shortly after our move to the Boston area, we enrolled him in the local kindergarten program with high hopes. While the first few years of elementary school were difficult, they were not unusual and no red flags were raised. After all, the children were given choices: "Would you rather play with blocks, draw a picture, or practice your letters?" One guess which activity our little "Lego builder" chose.

Flexibility exists in the early years of elementary education in the United States. While some might applaud this level of flexibility and others might criticize it, it was present in both of the schools my children attended in different school districts. One argument for allowing the children choice is that children mature and learn at different rates from each other, as well as at different rates across subjects. In fact, the second grade teacher pointed out the disparity in my son's skill-levels; he was "brilliant" in math and problem-solving and could read like a "whiz," but lagged behind in spelling and writing. We agreed on tutoring as a solution and, in addition, the teacher volunteered her *own* time twice a week before school; she understood that children respond differently to alternative learning environments and structures, and that children should not be limited to a single model. In fact, according to Thom Hartmann, author of *The Edison Gene*[1] (so named, because Thomas Edison is widely believed to have been hyperactive):

> *While a number of our schools emphasize rote memorization and test-taking, the real world rarely demands these as primary skills. ... The fact is, very few careers require sitting in one place for hours a day, switching topics every hour or two, although our schools seem locked into this as their singular model of education. ... One result can be that the child who functions differently is criticized or condemned for her[his] learning style. (p. 111)*

We were fortunate that both my son's second and third grade teachers seemed to understand and appreciate the variety of learning styles in children. Our son proved to be a quick learner and by third grade, his spelling was "at grade level." Although characterized as "immature" and "a bit overactive and fidgety in the classroom," we were told that he was *not* the most active child in the class. We remained optimistic about our son's continued progress and agreed to monitor his learning situation. A short time later we decided to move to Europe.

In sharing my experiences in educating our son in Holland, I am indebted to the advice provided by multiple researchers. Many of these doctors and parents have dedicated their lives to improving the educational system's response to children with a high energy level, and have written outstanding books for parents interested in improving the educational environment and experience for active children.[1-6]

While writing about my experiences does have a cathartic effect, I share my personal trials here to provide a source of comfort to other families who move overseas with an energetic child, and who might benefit from alternative teaching methods.

The news of our moving to Europe was greeted with enthusiasm by our son. After all, an adventurous child is always looking for new territories to explore and conquer. He insisted on packing his own clothes and belongings—music to a mother's ears! He carefully took apart each of his 50 Lego structures, separated each set into baggies, and placed their accompanying instructions inside. The largest and most complicated of his Lego sets he left built and packed meticulously in boxes, each surrounded by foam packing bubbles. My husband and I watched in amazement as X-wings, star fighters, ships, racing cars and forts all became carefully catalogued collections for future enjoyment.

Our first week in The Hague, Peter moved into his new room by carefully opening each baggie and rebuilding every Lego set! All indications were that this outgoing, risk-taking and daring child was going to embrace life and schooling in Europe with his usual energy and enthusiasm.

Dealing with a private school that is inflexible and rigid presents new challenges.

We optimistically packed his lunch for his first day at The American School of The Hague and introduced him to his new teacher and classmates. Upon overhearing the girls in his class whisper to each other that "the new boy at school was cute," I became confident that this year would be a positive experience for our son and that he would easily make new friends.

That confidence was short-lived. Soon we began to hear stories that he was expressing frustration in the classroom. We told ourselves that this was because he was overwhelmed by the transition to a foreign country. After all, we ourselves were struggling to cope. But after six weeks in his new school, we received a phone call for an early parent-teacher conference.

Although armed with multiple reasons why a young boy might have difficulties adjusting to a new school in the middle of a school year, I could not help but feel embarrassed and defensive; after all, he was my son. I had read enough to know that the structure and spirit of a household has a direct impact on the attitude of a child. If my son's temperament was unusual and non-conforming, then I was obviously an inadequate mother and disciplinarian. (Of course, there was also the ten years of "Mommy Guilt," because I had been a working mom, and not just a working mom, but also a deadline-junkie!) I had always been a proponent of "quality time" and he seemed to enjoy his after-school activities. But perhaps if I had spent more time with him, I could have changed him…

My first meeting with his teacher in Holland was similar to the following:

Teacher: *Your son seems to be a bright child.*

Me: *Yes, we are proud of him and he likes math.*

Teacher: *However, he is having a difficult time during group time.*

Me: *Well, we just moved here. Isn't this expected?*

Teacher: *For a few weeks, yes. But all of these other children have moved here in the past few years. It is my experience that an expatriate child should settle down within one month of the move.*

Me: *Well, it may take our son a little longer than most children—this has been a big transition for him.*

Teacher: *This has been a transition for all the children and he is making group time difficult...also, I have noticed he has difficulty with handwriting.*

Me: *Yes, he does have a history of difficulty with handwriting and spelling. But in the past we have handled this with tutoring and extra help from the teacher.*

Teacher: *I don't have time to give extra help to any child. In my classroom, each child must perform at the required grade level in every subject.*

I can remember feeling resentful following this meeting. How could a teacher *not* have extra time for a child in her classroom? How can each and every one of the twenty-one children perform at the same level? Why did this expensive private American School (which the corporations and embassies pay for) have no support structure for children with learning difficulties? Where were the tutors and caring teachers I was accustomed to? I was just beginning to realize the multiple drawbacks of an overseas private educational system that was not bound by recent American laws nor bound by local Dutch laws.

Our son became increasingly less happy and more resistant to attending school. We blamed *ourselves* for his lack of responsiveness and responsibility and we blamed *him* for his lack of focus and motivation in school. Thus, our son seemed angry at the world for its lengthy list of rules, regulations and requirements for a nine-year old boy: a new school, new teachers, new bus routes (where all children between the ages of 5 and 18 rode the bus together), and a new hockey team (where his teammates and coaches spoke a different language). While he liked the social aspect of school and he continued to perform at "above grade level" in mathematics and reading, he found the typical school day boring and frustrating.

Naturally, my son's dilemma was an additional source of stress. How could I help alter his temperament? How could I increase his motivation at school? Had we made a mistake moving overseas? We thought we were practicing good and progressive parenting by exposing the children to other cultures.

Some emotional relief came from the results of educational tests; our son's IQ was high. His performance, particularly in the areas of problem-solving and reading, was as high as a child two years older might be expected to perform. This was wonderful news and confirmed our anecdotal evidence of his academic strengths. The test also revealed that his writing skills lagged behind his age group. No surprise. The final conclusion of the test was that our son was under-performing at a level expected for his IQ.

The months that followed were among the most difficult for us and for our son. While Peter may indeed have been active, inattentive, and distractible, he had always been our "happy camper." We had enjoyed listening to his whistling all day, his singing in the shower, and even his early attempts at stand-up comedy. During this transitional period in the Netherlands, there was no whistling, no singing, no joke telling, no laughing, and very little smiling in our house. Where was our happy child?

The following school year we thought we were more prepared. As a result of the testing, our son was hand-placed with the most disciplined and demanding teacher in the grade. Unfortunately, unbeknownst to us, this teacher was also the least motivating; the results were debilitating and Peter was given no additional help by this teacher—or the school.

Although the school offered no assistance, either during or after hours, they were a believer in meeting to *talk* about the situation. We were surprised when we walked into the first meeting to find no less than ten people in the room! The principal, the counselor, the teacher, the language specialist, the speech specialist, the special education coordinator, the educational psychologist, the school nurse, myself, and my husband. My first thought was *My God, if this many people spent this much time discussing my daughter's self-esteem, she would have the ego of a surgeon by now!*

The school year progressed unevenly. We followed-up on several recommendations that were presented to us by the "committee," but none of them seemed to be effective. After exhausting our resources, our energy, and the attention of our son, who was now beginning to feel like a research specimen, we decided to take back control of the decision-making process. We were mystified that the school was unresponsive and did not seem to understand that different students have different learning styles. As Thom Hartmann so appropriately wrote in the *Edison Gene*[1]:

> *An Edison-gene child faces a double whammy in that he's also confronted with a school system that says he must fit in with the teaching and testing style in common use in order to be accepted. Failure and the blame associated with it ...can produce a stress-driven cortisol response... The result is that the child's intellectual development is slowed—which produces more stress that further slows the process of brain growth, which leads to more developmental delays. ... It's the result of the mismatch between his learning style and the school's teaching style, and doesn't have to happen. (p. 113)*

As a mother of a child labeled "impulsive and inattentive" in a rigid, inflexible school system, I have accepted that I will have different perspectives than other mothers. I know that mothers of girls who behave perfectly and primly never receive a call from the teacher or the principal, and have no understanding of my situation. I have been known to secretly cast a spell on them, so their next children will be overactive boys!

Match the technique of the teacher or coach with the learning style of the student.

Peter responds better to structure and clear boundaries and expectations. He does not respond well to transitions, lengthy periods of inactivity, and large group situations. He has had amazing success in classes that employ "self-paced" programs and positive reinforcement. His Dutch teacher actually used the term "natural linguist" to describe him. We accept that not all teachers and coaches use training methods that are consistent with my son's learning methods. For example, one tennis instructor declared our son unproductive and uncoachable, while another instructor declared him a future tennis star.

Despite the experimentation and frustration, our son has high self-esteem and is an optimistic individual. In the States, he was active athletically, so during our time abroad he joined an American soccer team, a Dutch tennis club, and a Dutch hockey league in Leiden. He eventually learned to understand the local language through a combination of school instruction, time with our neighbors, and Dutch TV and movies. An incentive to learn Dutch may have been his inability to join in "locker-room banter" and the fact that his hockey coach spoke two languages, neither of which was English.

I have only recently learned, and am still learning, to accept that Peter's temperament is different. He falls in the minority of students who might be considered overactive, even though some sources estimate that as many as 15% of all elementary school boys may exhibit above "normal" activity levels. Some researchers hypothesize that while girls may also exhibit hyperactivity, the manifestations are different, so their behavior is often attributed to other causes and given alternative labels. In fact, this estimate of 15% is not surprising if a child's activity or attention level follows a normal distribution, and if "normal" is restricted to the middle 70% of the activity range.

Once we understood that the learning structure at the school was only suitable for the middle range of students, and that our son was not alone in this "mismatch of methods," we were better able to appreciate our son's natural gifts. Peter is funny, witty, outgoing, caring and conscientious. He makes us laugh. He is determined and passionate. He draws us into his enthusiasm. He is a risk-taker. He amazes us with his willingness to try new activities. He is intense. He astounds us with his meticulous knowledge of historical facts. He is bright. He surprises us with his "non-linear" thinking. He is athletic and continues to amaze us with his skill and energy on the field and on the court. And we are proud of his accomplishments.

Raising Peter has been an exhilarating experience as we realize how enthusiastic, inventive and innovative he can be. In fact, as Thom Hartmann[1] noted:

> *I and many scientists, educators, physicians, and therapists believe that when these unique children don't succeed in ... schools, it's often because of a disconnect between them—their brains are wired to make them brilliant inventors and entrepreneurs—and our schools, which are set up for children whose brains are wired to make them good workers in the structured environments of a factory or office cubicle. (p. 5)*

What I have learned from my experiences with an overseas education is that selecting the appropriate school for a child is not easy, particularly in a foreign country; relying on websites and reports from the relocation consultant is not sufficient. Also, although location is one priority, perhaps it should not be the *top* priority, while admitting that logistics cannot be ignored. Multiple factors should play a role in the decision-making process, to help ensure that the overseas experience is positive for your child.

As a result of surviving an imperfect private learning environment, I recommend that expatriates remain as stringent in selecting an overseas school as they would be in evaluating school districts or private institutions when they make a move in their home country. My mistake was making the assumption that an American School would follow American standards and would by default be the best place for our son.

In addition to disappointment with the support mechanisms and lack of teacher involvement, we discovered that the maturity level of the children (mostly expatriate corporate or embassy children) at an overseas American school is accelerated; a potential issue if the child is new to the expatriate community. Dutch children were a better match for my son's maturity level and, in fact, his best friend at The American School was a Dutch boy, one of the few local children at the school.

As a final note, Dr. Lucy Jo Palladino in her book entitled *Dreamers, Discoverers, & Dynamos*[4] (formerly entitled *The Edison Trait*) focuses on the positive perspective of raising an active or impulsive child. She provides the reader with useful information, while still encouraging reliance on individual choices. She promotes the adaptation to new learning methods, experimentation with treatments, and most importantly, pride for the potential creativity, ingenuity and energy contained in your "Edison trait child." This book should be required reading for all educators at all levels of our educational system.

Dr. Palladino suggests encouraging your child's interests and coaching your child in self-achievement to emphasize their role as a learner, participator and contributor in life. [4] While not all families have a child that is a "dynamo," most children have different learning styles and different learning rates. Therefore, in preparation for moving to a different cultural and academic environment and for selecting the most appropriate educational program for a child, I suggest the following:

One:	Trust your own instincts.
Two:	Interview potential schools.
Three:	Play an active role in teacher selection.
Four:	Talk to other parents.
Five:	Listen to your child.
Six:	Encourage learning of the local language.
Seven:	Encourage membership in local clubs.
Eight:	Foster friendships.

NOTES

Chapter 8: Educating a Dynamo

1. Hartmann, Thom (2003), *The Edison Gene: ADHD and the Gift of the Hunter Child*, Rochester, Vermont: Park Street Press.
2. Garber, S.W. Barber, M.D. and R. F. Spizman (1996), *Beyond Ritalin*, New York: HarperCollins Publishers.
3. Hallowell, E.M. and John J. Ratey (1994), *Driven to Distraction: Recognizing and Coping with Attention Deficit Disorder from Childhood through Adulthood*, New York: Pantheon Books.
4. Palladino, Lucy Jo (1999), *Dreamers, Discoverers & Dynamos*, New York: Ballantine Books.
5. Reichenberg-Ullman J. and Robert Ullman (2000), *Ritalin-Free Kids: Safe and Effective Homeopathic Medicine for ADHD and other Learning Problems*, New York: Random House, Inc.
6. Turecki, Stanley (2000), *The Difficult Child*, 2nd revised paperback edition, New York: Bantam Books.

Zo moeder, zo dochter.

Like mother, like daughter.

Chapter 9

Raising a Daughter

Why is it that mothers and daughters have a difficult time simply being in the same room, particularly if this room is the kitchen? My own mother and I have a long history of approaching self-combustion if we spend more than a few days together. A typical visit from my parents unfolds as follows:

Day 1: We lovingly greet each other like kindred spirits and are dismayed at the stretch of time we have allowed to pass between visits.

Day 2: We catch up on family news. Comments are made on the behavior of my children. (Matchstick #1) We spend the day together walking, shopping and visiting museums. Complaints are mumbled that we walk too far, don't select the appropriate lunch place, and visit expensive museums filled with distasteful modern art. (Matchstick #2) We return home starving, still glowing from our active day and attempt to cook the evening meal together. Chefs compete in the kitchen over the correct portions of basil and garlic, the proper balanced meal for the children, and the appropriate recipe to follow, or as in my husband's case, the fact that he uses no recipe. (Matchstick #3)

Day 3: We rise for breakfast. Our coffee is too strong and our bacon too crispy. Judgments are made and words are shared about the disintegration of discipline. The volume escalates. The bonfire begins. Soon our neighbors know the intimate details of our family frustrations. My father wisely decides it is time that he and my mother leave.

The Dutch have a saying that *Gasten en vissen blijven maar drie dagen goed.*

The English translation of this Dutch adage is equally applicable across the Atlantic; "Guests and fish are only good for three days." The lack of longevity of both guests and fish has nothing to do with how we feel about them. I love fish and I love my mother, and not necessarily in that order.

My mother has been a wonderful mom. She quit teaching to raise my two brothers and me, and the three of us always came first. I have fond memories of my childhood, and of a safe and nurtured youth.

Given that I am hampered, or some say blessed, by a short memory, I grasp onto the few visions I feel slipping away and savor them. Lunches alone with mom devouring steaming plates of macaroni and asking her questions about my soon-to-be-born brother who was visibly making her tummy larger by the day. Downtown shopping trips to "help" my mom purchase new dresses, although my version of help was to crawl between the dressing rooms and report back on the taste of the other shoppers. Balmy summer evenings licking fast-melting, black-raspberry cones at Pat's Ice Cream Parlor—the preferred flavor of my dad. Autumn afternoons helping to rake endless clumps of leaves and then jumping headfirst into the grand heap, until mom yanked us out by our collars, scolding us that we would all end up with a head full of bugs, while we turned and sneaked in one last jump.

After I turned eleven my childhood ended, as it does for many girls. This phase of puberty was sudden and unrelenting. The physical changes were early and unforgiving, and yet my mother never changed. She continued to be a source of comfort and compassion.

It was mom who defended me when my brothers called me "fat-hippo," since I no longer had the figure of a "string-bean." It was mom, who patiently listened to silly squabbles with girlfriends and then helped to plot the forgive-and-forget strategies. It was mom who watched me shed countless tears during traumatic break-ups (most of which are long forgotten) and then proceeded to explain why none of them were worthy of me. Mom was always there when I needed her...So what changes the relationship between mothers and daughters? Daughters grow up.

My daughter was born when I was 28 years old, while I was repaying my school loans, learning about married life, and still enjoying being an underpaid and overworked researcher. Although we had been trying to have a child, my pregnancy was a bit unexpected. (We thought it would take twelve months to conceive—instead it took twelve minutes!)

While *we* were overjoyed, my boss was less than thrilled, after all, she had delayed having *her* child until she had successfully earned tenure. What was I thinking? Who was I to believe the stories that mothers could also have careers?

New mothers and new careers are a challenging combination.

My decision (or really, my husband's set of fast swimming sperm) was not popular. So, I dug in my heels and began the tradition of working to prove myself…to prove that my being pregnant would not impact my work; to prove that I could write just as many articles as my male colleagues; and to prove that my boss had hired the best person for the job. Throughout my pregnancy, I continued to show up at my office at the university every morning—including the day I went into labor.

Although my long-term memory has a short-term expiration date, some things, such as the pain of childbirth, are never forgotten. After 30 hours of prolonged suffering, way too many ice chips in my mouth, an eventual drugged state (only after the patients in the next wing complained they could hear my screams), and the use of forceps to turn the baby (my husband called them "giant salad spoons"), our little angel entered this world.

She was perfect. I was still in a stupefied state, but they told me she was physically healthy. She was crying and needy. I was petrified and dependent on, of all people, my mother. The baby did not come with a set of instructions about feeding, bathing, holding and caring. How unfair. My friends had told me that once I gave birth, my "mothering instincts" would kick in and I would know exactly what to do. Well, no instincts surfaced, other than crying, and the only thing kicking was the baby!

My mother stayed one week to care for the two of us and then departed, leaving behind only a verbal list of do's and don'ts. I remember crying when my mother left. I was ill equipped and ill prepared. Just like all new mothers, I was exhausted and overwhelmed. I could barely manage the stairs myself, let alone while balancing a new baby, the receiving blanket and the bassinet! This was a time (perhaps the only time) I wished that my mother still lived with me, or at least close enough to drop by and share her nuggets of advice over coffee.

Despite juggling work, a baby, and a new Labrador puppy, we all seemed to adjust and adopt the ways of proud, new parents. Only 100% cotton cloth diapers were permitted to touch her skin and I nursed her faithfully. Although, even as a nursing mother, I was never well endowed, and the milk pumps quickly ran dry.

Of course, she was the smartest baby in New Haven. She walked first, talked first, and even learned to use the potty first. No "nappies" for this toddler. At six weeks she accompanied me to a conference at my Alma Mater; at three months we introduced her to the family island, where she didn't find the lack of plumbing a problem; and at 10 months we whisked her off to the beaches of Key West. She toddled, clapped her hands and smiled gleefully for every toddler photo; even the candid shots reflected images of an outgoing and confident child. We observed no sign of the future self-doubting, self-judging, peer-dependent, and mother-averse teenager lurking inside.

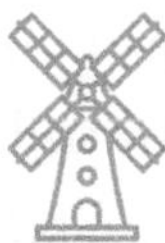

Despite our move to Maine and juggling less-than-perfect day-care situations, our daughter Katrina continued to thrive and grow into an enthusiastic and active child. She enjoyed trips to our cabin, where she now regarded the lack of plumbing as a fun expedition to the "out-house." She basked in the glory of being an only child, and an only grandchild, with attention bestowed on her by proud parents, two adoring uncles, two still childless aunts, and three sets of grandparents. Not a demand was unmet, not a cry was unanswered, and not a hug was unreturned. This was her moment in "I-am-an-only-child" heaven.

Our daughter's own private Eden disappeared when her brother was born. Even prior to his entry into this world, she had to live with less attention; my pregnancy was difficult and ended with two months of complete bed rest. From the womb, our son was already demanding top billing! The doctor's orders to spend more time on my back meant less time for walks in the park and fewer visits to the playground with my daughter. I grew to rely heavily on neighbors.

Surprisingly, the arrival of our son was easy and painless. He arrived on the scene almost effortlessly, eager to see what he had been missing during his weeks of confinement (although, I can't imagine that my hours of watching Red Sox baseball during my bed rest enticed him into this world).

Our son was so anxious to make his appearance that my husband nearly missed it. Assuming this would be another 30-hour delivery, I had purposely delayed putting out the SOS call, thinking we had time to spare. Upon his arrival to the hospital, he was thrown a pair of scrubs and rushed into the delivery room. Thirty minutes later we had a son, with no screams and no drugs.

Within a few hours of the blessed event, our daughter was eagerly introduced to her brother Peter with a teddy bear as her first peace offering. She was excited to peer at the newest member of the family with the tiny fingers, baby-powder smell, and pale complexion.

Her brother was a dream baby and reeled us in. His sleeping periods seemed to extend with no end, in fact, we frequently woke him because we were concerned he was over-sleeping. Of course, if we had known what lay ahead, we would have let him sleep all day! Our daughter's Garden of Eden was still intact, yet fragile, and her claim to center stage slowly slipped away. The leading role was grabbed by her understudy, initially by an exploring toddler, and ultimately by an impulsive and aggressive boy. There was no return to paradise for our girl; at least not the same paradise.

It is so easy to meet the demands of an assertive child at the expense of a less demanding sibling that it took us years to realize what was happening in our family. The personality of our daughter was changing before our eyes. Her competition and battles with her brother grew as her self-confidence and self-assurance diminished. Whether this ongoing sibling rivalry naturally developed because of the gender disparity and age difference, or was exacerbated by intensive demands of an overactive brother, we do not know.

While an aggressive sibling may be more distracting, we believe that that our daughter's reaction to our son's ability to maintain center stage has been compounded by the gender difference. She may have even inferred that the gender difference *was* the reason for the change. After all, our culture promotes the preference for *male* athletic events, *male* political figures (yes, she has repeatedly asked why there has never been a woman president), and *male* career-focused marriages. As Barbara Mackoff states in *Growing a Girl*, "socialization creates sex differences." [1]

How can we counteract the influences of cultural gender images on our daughter? Our different expectations for our son versus our daughter may have contributed to her self-image. Perhaps, our preoccupation and participation with our son's soccer and hockey leagues was natural for her to expect; a result of having a *brother*, rather than a result of having an inattentive and impulsive sibling.

It is clear that adolescent girls struggle with challenges and pressures during this period of self-awareness.

Although not unique to girls, adolescence is a difficult period of development. While girls have faced the pressures of puberty since the beginning of time, there is a dearth of studies and publications on adolescence. In contrast, while the diagnosis of hyperactivity disorders in young children is relatively recent, trips to the local bookstore (both in the U.S. and in the Netherlands) revealed entire aisles of literature on the hyperactivity phenomenon, focusing on the misunderstood child, the under-performing boy, the impulsive son, the inattentive dreamer, or the over-active under-achiever. The results of a similar search for help with a troubled adolescent girl paled in comparison. Should we believe that most girls *glide* through this "privileged" period of their lives?

On the contrary, the acclaimed documentary of adolescent lives by Mary Pipher entitled, *Reviving Ophelia: Saving the Selves of Adolescent Girls*, reveals an alarming array of issues for this age group.[2] According to Pipher, puberty is a period of pain, pathology and problems. It is a time for self-judging, self-doubting and self-blaming. Between the ages of 11 and 15, the seeds of delinquency and depression are planted, and the roots of anti-socialism, sexism, sexual abuse, alcoholism, drug addiction and eating disorders gain strength.

Adolescence is when dreams take shape and self-esteem solidifies. Beyond the boundaries of the family are the unrelenting images on television, videos, and Internet of our cultural image of girls and women, thus making the treatment of our daughters, granddaughters, and nieces within the protective growth of our family tree that much more critical.

While as a mother, I have always had good intentions in the raising of my children, I'm afraid that I have fallen into the much-feared trap of becoming like *my* mother—something I swore would never happen. As Dr. Pipher so aptly explains in her chapter on the relationship between daughters and mothers:

> *Growing up requires adolescent girls to reject the person with whom they are most closely identified. Daughters are socialized to have a tremendous fear of becoming like their mothers. There is no greater insult for most women than to say, "You are just like your mother." And yet to hate one's mother is to hate oneself.*[3]

I have adopted many of the same habits and characteristics of my mother that I disliked when I was an adolescent. Unfortunately, I am critical of my daughter's clothes, behavior and choices. We disagree and argue about style, sports, television and social decisions. The more I advise, the more my daughter resists. And if a childhood friend had witnessed my recent discussions with my daughter, I have no doubt that she would have declared, "You are just like your mother!"

Perhaps we should resign ourselves to the fact that we all do eventually become a bit like our mothers, and that we all feel as Mary Pipher does:

> *My relationship with my mother…was extraordinarily complex, filled with love, longing, a need for closeness and distance, separation and fusion. I respected her and mocked her, felt ashamed and proud of her, laughed with her and felt irritated by her smallest flaws. I felt*

crabby after twenty-four hours in her house, and yet nothing made me happier than making her happy.[4]

We know that our move to the Netherlands has provided an impetus for change in our priorities. In analyzing and documenting how dramatically all of our lives changed as a result of our living overseas, we became greater proponents of change. Although prior to our move, many of our friends had warned that displacing a child during her adolescent years may be "bad timing," we have discovered that inducing change during this critical stage of development was, in fact, *perfect* timing.

How has our move to Holland improved my awareness of my relationship with my daughter? What have we learned from our time among different cultures?

The main advantage of moving—and particularly moving overseas—can be stated in one word: *change.*

Moving encourages change. For our daughter, this meant change in her peer group, change in her choices, change in our family structure, and change in our relationship. Change is difficult, yet necessary. Change is challenging, yet compelling. Change can open doors and opportunities. As Irene Dunlap so aptly wrote in one of the few books for pre-adolescents, *Chicken Soup for the Preteen Soul*:[5]

Change is the only absolute
in the world,
the only thing

that you can depend on.
Nothing stays the same.
Tomorrow will come,
bringing with it
new beginnings and sometimes
unexpected endings.
You can hold on to the past
and get left in the dust;
or, you can choose to
jump on the ride of life
and live a new adventure
with perseverance and
an open mind.

Moving overseas has been an impetus for change...an opportunity to renew bonds within our family, Newly-forged bonds, dented and damaged bonds, and even long-forgotten bonds, once thought too battered and broken to repair. Although we had always been a close family, we had become fragmented in recent years. My work addiction and self-absorption, Peter's frequent traveling, the school meetings for our son, and our ultimate necessity to focus on our own relationship left little time to work on an equally important part of our lives—our relationship with our daughter. Moreover, in Holland, our standard support network was over 3000 miles away.

In the absence of family members and peers, mothers and daughters turn toward each other.

When a family moves abroad, at first there is nobody else. There is no best friend to chat with, no nurturing neighbor to run to, and no school buddies to rely on. This sense of isolation during the initial phase in a foreign country is profound.

All we had was each other. If we wanted a confidant, a supportive shoulder, a lending hand, or a familiar face, we had little choice, but to turn to one another.

Thus, my pre-adolescent daughter was willing, perhaps even motivated, to spend time with her ancient (and most often embarrassing) mother. My daughter and I spent mornings sharing stories, afternoons sampling local shops, evenings viewing films at the local *bioscoop* and weekends visiting museums.

It was my chance to enjoy the last few years with my daughter before she became a full-blown teenager (with even less interest in her mother). It was my daughter's chance to revel in the undivided attention of a non-guilt-ridden, non-working mother.

Living across the Atlantic had other unforeseen advantages. The lack of external influence from family and friends allowed us to focus internally on our own needs, without offending the all-important and well-meaning three sets of in-laws.

If we wanted to travel to a foreign city, we left town for a week. If we wanted to bike to the local beach, we cycled all day. If we wanted to spend an entire weekend alone with our children, we did. Our obligation to make, or not break, social engagements was diminished, as was our need to follow the rhythmic beat of social climbers. We had a greater sense of control over our time outside of school and work. We had fewer intrusions in our lives, and fewer pressures to conform and participate.

Not surprisingly, the proximity of unique (but not necessarily popular) travel destinations pulled at the nomad in each of us. These trips provided a terrific opportunity to spend time alone with my daughter. I learned more about her during these brief journeys than I did during all her years in primary school. These mother-daughter solo times offered glimpses into her soul.

During our time abroad, I witnessed her eye-filled wonder during Easter morning service at a post-World War II church in Berlin, where she spent her time admiring magnificent stained glass windows, since she could not understand the German hymns. I observed her intense interest in the masterpieces of impressionist artists at the Van Gogh Museum in Amsterdam and the Musee d'Orsay in Paris, where she would not allow me to skip a single piece of artwork, although we had been there for hours and I was practically sleep-walking.

I watched her question and critique the detail, style and color of the clothing collection at the V & A Museum in London as she privately wondered what she would look like in the trendy evening gowns and laughed out loud at the mod "twiggy" fashions of the 60s. (While we were discussing fashion, her brother and father were viewing the world's largest ant farm at The Natural History Museum, to satisfy their self-proclaimed interest in ants over art.) Nothing can replace time alone with a child—particularly with an adolescent daughter.

Moving provides an opportunity to define a different peer group.

As our daughter made friends in Holland, she naturally began to choose time with her friends over time with her mother. While this was a difficult realization for me, it was a healthy and necessary show of independence. In addition, her new peer group was anything but traditional; her new friends at the British School were from all corners of the world—England, South Africa, Australia, Croatia, Ireland and Holland. As a result of their international experience and frequent exposure to change, Katrina discovered that they were *more* accepting of differences and *less* vulnerable to peer pressures than a homogeneous group.

As my daughter has matured and developed changes in priorities, peers, and preferences, we have grown closer. We have leaned on each other during times of transition and turmoil, and our social and political views have converged. As other mothers can agree, it's a joy to witness your daughter move beyond the teenage years and develop her own philosophies and perspectives as she launches her academic and professional career.

Although raising a girl is difficult, our time outside of our hometown-box enabled me to focus on my daughter's feelings more completely, to listen to her concerns more attentively, to observe her positive attributes more easily, to see her dreams more clearly, and to participate in her life more enthusiastically. As a result of spending time with my daughter and observing the impact of change as she has matured, I have renewed hope in relationships between mothers and daughters. For modern mothers, new books continue to shed light and share advice on how to raise a daughter.[6–8]

NOTES

Chapter 9: Raising a Daughter

1. Mackoff, Barbara (1996), *Growing A Girl*, New York: Dell Publishing.
2. Pipher, Mary (1994), *Reviving Ophelia: Saving the Selves of Adolescent Girls*, New York: Ballantine Books.
3. Ibid, p. 103.
4. Pipher, p. 102.
5. Canfield, J., Hansen, M.V., Hansen, P., and Irene Dunlap (2000), *Chicken Soup for the Preteen Soul*, Deerfield Beach: Health Communications, Inc.
6. Dobson, J. (2010), *Bringing Up Girls: Practical Advice and Encouragement for those Shaping the Next Generation of Women*, Carol Stream, IL: Tyndale House Publishers, Inc.
7. Elium, D. and J. Elium (2003), *Raising a Daughter: Parents and the Awakening of a Healthy Woman*, Berkeley, CA: Celestial Arts.
8. Meeker, Meg (2019), *Raising a Strong Daughter in a Toxic Culture: 11 Steps to Keep Her Happy, Healthy, and Safe*, Washington, DC: Regnery Publishing.

Het mes snijdt aan twee kante.

It cuts both ways.

Chapter 10

To Stay or Not to Stay?

One evening, while we were packing for our return trip to the States, my husband walked through the door after work promptly at six o'clock, parked his bicycle in the garden, and asked if I had any interest in *un*packing. I stopped mincing, turned off my favorite BBC program (a cooking show with time-saving tips), and sat down. My first thought was: here we go again.

Peter: *The good news is that our daughter would be able to finish high school here.*

Me: *Why?*

Peter: *The surprising news is that I have an offer to remain in The Hague.*

Me: *What do you mean?!*

Peter: *My company has another opening here—this would be a great opportunity for me.*

Me: *What about our plans to return to the States?*

Peter: *I know, but…*

Me: *But, what?*

Peter: *Just think...we could remain in Europe and continue traveling.*

Me: *Yes, the rail system is great here...but what about the children's schooling?*

Peter: *Our children's education would be paid for and I could continue biking to work.*

Me: *Yes, I do like your commute here...but what about our families?*

Peter: *Well, I know you would miss your mom, but you wouldn't have to say 'goodbye' to our neighbors.*

Peter really knew how to hit below the belt. He knew that although I enjoy the fresh flowers, the local cheese, and the city life, it is the neighborhood I would miss the most.

In particular, it was my neighbor and new-found friend, Marie Louise: the woman who introduced me to Dutch art (from Rembrandt to Mondrian), Dutch politics (from social legislation to Royal weddings), and Dutch cooking (from *erwtensoep* to *zuurkool pastei*), who I would miss the most. She adopted a *buitenlander* without reservation, suffered my early attempts at her language, and guided me on the *fietspaden* of The Hague. After a while, I didn't mind that our cycle excursions ended at nude beaches, even though I lost all hope of developing those well-shaped Dutch legs!

I would miss our Irish friends—*vrolijke vrienden*, who greeted everyone with a smile, a song, a hug, and eternal optimism—the kind that can only come from globetrotting for Royal Dutch Shell. They were generous and giving and never seemed discouraged by the countless challenges and changes encountered by an expatriate family. We will never forget the meter-long Noordzee salmon they grilled as a special send-off, complete with eyes and gaping mouth!

I would miss Maureen, a former Dutch model struggling to raise two boys on her own. We shared tea once a week, while she corrected my pronunciation and pathetic attempts at local proverbs. She worried about my stress level and gave me advice on the powers of homeopathic medicine for ulcers and headaches. If only I had known her before our time abroad!

I would miss the impromptu language lessons from Willi at the *bloemenwinkel* and I would miss the patience of Stephanie, who learned how to cut my hair through creative hand gestures. I would miss the entire family at the corner Indonesian restaurant, Tony at the local pizza parlor, and Wanda at the *Italiaanse winkel*, each of whom patiently listened as I practiced my Dutch, then responded with a smile; they too remembered what it was like to arrive in Holland and struggle with the guttural accent.

I would miss the *Hollandse kaas*, the giant stalks of garlic, 22 varieties of brown bread, 52 flavors of yogurt, and a seemingly endless variety of inexpensive, yet high-quality, French wine—all within a five-minute bike ride. I would miss the lack of commercials, the access to news in five languages, and the absence of commercialism during holidays; there were no Hallmark ads in February and no giant dancing bunnies in April. I would miss the lengthy vacations and visits to chateaus and the Champs Elysees, only a few hours away by train. I would miss the towns of Locmariaquer and Larmor-Plage in Brittany, where one week at a seaside cottage was the same price as one night at a hotel on Martha's Vineyard.

I would miss the low humidity, lack of snow, and proximity of sand. Where else can one live in a major European *stad* and be seaside in 10 minutes by bike? I would miss the ancient architecture, abstract art, and trips to the Ardennes. I would miss the long Nordic skates (which are harder to use than they look), the whimsical, yet practical winches, the canal-side cafes, and the Royal processions through city streets, complete with horse-drawn carriages.

I would miss seeing the shocking *Nederlandse* orange color everywhere: orange *hutjes* on April 30th for Queen's Day, and orange faces painted by fanatical fans during *voetbal* matches. I would miss the cool beauty of *Delfts blauw* used in local tile, pottery and miniature collectibles, like those that fill the *poppenhuizen* on display at the Rijksmuseum. I would miss the stark white of the majestic modern windmills against the horizon of the Dutch countryside. (Why the U.S. is so resistant to this efficient form of energy defies logic.)

I would miss the sight of men playing field hockey, the national sport, and the attentiveness of the *politie*. I would miss the short bike ride to the supermarket, even if I often felt like a juggler balancing my wares. I would miss the easy rail ride to Schiphol, one of the largest international airports in the world. (What is wrong with American urban planners that they can't put rail stations at major airports?)

Beyond the physical conveniences, I would miss the less measurable advantages of time. Time to cook. Time to learn. Time to observe. Time to travel. Time to breathe. If we decided to return to the States, I would inevitably return to my obsession with work. Like an addict unable to resist, I would be drawn to the drama of the classroom and return to my workaholic ways. Would I be able to retain a balanced perspective?

I know that I have expanded my mind, broadened my opinions, and grown as an individual. More importantly, my relationship with my children has been nourished. We have learned to appreciate our similarities and understand our differences. Would we continue this mutual support? Could I avoid my old obsession with work? Could I balance the multiple roles of wife and mother with that of the independent dreamer that I had also taken on? I'm not sure that I am wiser, even though I am unmistakably and unfortunately older.

While living in Holland, I celebrated one of those milestone birthdays that end in a zero, although I would not admit to being this age, even to my doctor—as if he couldn't tell from my record—for at least three more years.

As I reflect on the years before we moved to Holland, I recall how difficult they were. Marital relationships take time, and time was something we did not have, or we did not make. Between the one dog, two kids, and the multiple career demands, we always seemed to be running or driving. Driving to work, driving to school, driving to appointments, driving to meetings, and just plain driving each other crazy. Early mornings. Lengthy commutes. Longer days. Less sleep. Play-dates. Politics. Pressure. Work. Work. Work.

After many years of servitude to the corporate craziness, we had seized the opportunity to escape to Europe in the hope of glimpsing a different way of life. To our surprise, we found it—in Holland. We were nurtured by the change and choices we found during our move abroad. And we discovered that we had control over our choices as we transitioned to a life with different priorities and a slower pace.

As we learned, change can be good. Change does not provide a cure—but a chance, an opportunity to reassess the value and consequence of choices. It is the beginning of the realization that everything we do *is* a choice; there is very little in life that is an obligation. From organizing activities for our children every waking hour, accepting every invitation, and giving the perfect lecture in every class, to saying "yes" to every invitation, how we spend our time and our energy is our choice.

Moving creates innumerable choices—and surprises. Where should we live? Where should our children attend school? Who would we spend time with? What would we do with our free time?

Before we arrived in The Hague, I predicted that I would take up gardening. (Those who know me, please stop laughing!) Like cooking, I had never devoted any attention to learning the names, colors, habits and growing requirements of plants. Just as I was known for the color of my bacon (black), I was also known for the color of my thumb (brown).

In The Hague, our home had a large enclosed garden with several beautiful rose bushes and several other perennials, which I learned blossomed every year without new bulb plantings. I was surprised and pleased at the existence of something that will flower and prosper each year without much nurturing.

I imagined myself ensconced in colorful books detailing the history and horticulture of roses, planting new varieties, and designing my own version of a victory garden. But as the months passed, the most I could manage were geraniums in clay pots. Instead of figuring out why my roses never bloomed, my tulips never lasted, and other plants never grew at all, I returned to the classroom in Holland—only this time as a student—and discovered that I liked it. I enjoyed sitting side-by-side with students eager and motivated to learn; each from a different country with a unique perspective. Instead of gardening, I chose learning and traded in my trowel for tutoring. Instead of rose books, I chose Dutch grammar books. I made my choices, they were just different than I had imagined.

I had never enjoyed traveling before moving to Holland, at least not post-children. Traveling required packing, unpacking, washing, folding and ironing. (No, actually scratch that last one, since I never owned an iron.)

To me, traveling meant sleeping in strange beds, waking up at early hours, quieting screaming kids on the plane, hoping we hadn't forgotten anything, or that the airline wouldn't lose our bags, and keeping up with a pre-scheduled itinerary. Business trips were no better. Returning home meant catching up on laundry, dishes and sleep. Somehow, I had missed the romantic allure of traveling that others found appealing.

In Europe, traveling took on new meaning. Traveling by rail, cycle, or car gave us time. Time to talk and time to listen. Clearly, these were skills we had lost in our struggle for personal advancement and perfection.

We had not traveled more than a weekend without children since our honeymoon, which had been a wonderful three-week random tour through southern Europe with only a few Francs and Marks in our pockets. We slept in the car, stayed at cheap *pensions* and lived on bread, bratwurst and cheese. We drove where we wanted, visited who we wanted, and left when we wanted, once departing furtively at 3:00am because we felt safer on the road than in the cheap motel we had chosen in Rouen!

Although our trips during our stay in Holland were seldom spontaneous (not possible with a dog and two kids in tow), and we could now afford nicer accommodations (the European-traveler dog ate and slept better than we did on our honeymoon), they were reminiscent of the same adventurous and amorous spirit. The sites may have changed, but the sensation was the same: excitement and exhilaration.

Since we now involved our children in the choices; in addition to *brasseries*, *biergartens*, and beaches, we now visited places that were interactive and interesting for pre-teens. We visited each and every D-Day site (please just one more, mom!) on the coast of Normandy, complete with bunkers to climb on, and World War I battlefields in Belgium, complete with trenches to crawl through.

In addition to wandering the halls of the Louvre in Paris, we went window-shopping on the Champs Elysees for our daughter and survived the trek to the top of the Eiffel Tower for our son (although the glass elevators—never mind the vistas—were a bit much for those of us who are "altitude-challenged").

In London, we rode the giant London Eye and wandered the halls of torture at the wax museum. In Nuremberg, in addition to sipping beer from steins or *stiefel*, we enjoyed the *Spielzeug Museum*, home to the largest model train, which kept both my boys busy for hours. In Germany, we visited *Neuschwanstein*, the castle home of crazy Ludwig and the model for the Disney castle. The children liked it every bit as much as we did 15 years earlier.

For our family, these trips represented a major change. A change from routines and deadlines. A change from business travel. A change from commuting and working. A change from rushing and running. A change from underlying avoidance and arguments. The change was good.

We controlled our choices. We chose to engage in meaningful conversation, even if we were stuck in a 30-kilometer traffic jam. We chose to browse the local shops, even if we couldn't read the signs on the doors. We chose to cook more meals by ourselves, even if Peter was still better at it. We chose to ski as a family, even if the boys skied the black diamonds, while the girls skied the beginner slopes at Chamonix. We chose to take beach walks with the dog, even if it rained nearly everyday in winter. We chose to be together.

As the memories faded, Peter's voice resonated in my ears and brought me back to the present—with the aroma of garlic burning, once again.

Peter: *If you prefer, there is also the option of moving to a different city.*
Me: *Where?*
Peter: *London…*
Me: *Well, at least I wouldn't have to learn a different language.*
Peter: *…or Munich.*
Me: *OK, I could try to recapture my German.*
Peter: *We need to decide quickly.*
Me: *When?*
Peter: *Today.*

As luck would have it, we had already given up our brick, rose-covered haven in The Hague and a British family was set to move in next month. We had prepared the neighbors for our departure and signed a lease for a cottage on the coast of Brittany for the second straight summer, a place to pass the time while our goods were on the slow boat to Boston. If we stayed in The Netherlands, no places for the children in private schools had been reserved. Tryouts for local sports teams had long since passed. The wheels of moving were already in motion.

We had purchased a new house in the States and were preparing for the transition, although selecting our new home from overseas had been a challenge. I knew that a separation from my favorite *kaaswinkel* would be heartbreaking, so prior to our return to the States, we conducted a full-scale search of the delis in the Boston suburbs to find the one that carried the greatest variety of Dutch cheese. I instructed our realtor to find us a home within a 10-minute radius of the chosen cheese shop. Some people choose their town based on schools, we chose ours based on cheese *and* schools!

More importantly, not returning to the States would mark the end of my career, at least an academic one. I had agreed (reluctantly) to return to teaching and course assignments had already been made for the fall. Perhaps my new appreciation for change and balance in life could be imported and improve my teaching abilities, even if the subject of study bore little resemblance to learning a new language or burrowing through bunkers. Could I successfully return to the classroom? Could I still motivate, encourage, and educate students?

I didn't know, but we decided I should try. We wanted to find out if it is possible for us to both work and still value our time, our children and our solitude. We wanted our lessons learned to become our mantras, our motivations—not merely memories. We wanted to discover if we could keep growing closer together, and maintain two careers. So, I said, "Let's go home!"

My gaze wandered around the kitchen, which had been the center of my journey to discovering new tastes and smells. I can still recall the pungent odor of cherries steeped in wine—delicious, but oh so potent. On the surface, the kitchen seemed ordinary: the black and white tile floor where Mickie liked to lay on warm days to stay cool, the oversized white porcelain sink where I had broken my share of glasses, and the gas range, where I had finally overcome my fears of sautéeing, simmering and basting.

At the back of the kitchen, double French doors led out to an enclosed rose garden, our private haven from the sounds of the *stad*, and just spacious enough for wine or tea with Marie Louise. The sounds of glasses clinking, her girls giggling, and dangling Dutch phrases still hung in the air. We had grown accustomed to the lack of screens (not generally found in Europe), so the doors were typically left wide open, allowing any stray or sudden burst of sunshine to enter the house in full force.

Upstairs, I had made a daily habit of lounging in the antique claw-foot tub (perfect for soaking soles aching from pounding pavement). We all had improved our legs on multiple daily trips up and down the four flights of narrow stairs (no StairMaster needed here), although the hope of gaining the physique of the shapely Dutch cycling legs was put to rest.

I would be leaving all this—and more—behind, not knowing when I would return.

Finally, I wondered, now that we had finally invested the time in and improved our relationship, would it survive a return to the frantic American work ethic? (Alas, if only the separatists had spent more time in Leiden with the merrymaking Dutch!) What would change when we returned? As I have witnessed, change can be good, but is it possible to hold fast onto the positive and change only the negative?

Not all questions are meant to have answers. That's why we take risks, and it appeared that we were going to take another one.

We finished the packing, survived the movers (easier the second time around), sold our Opel to Maureen, un-enrolled as Dutch residents at the town hall (otherwise you pay fees forever), loaded a rented van (crowned by King Mickie one last time), and waved a lingering goodbye to the neighbors, who were all out on the street to send us off. With a shower of kisses, shouts of *Dag*! and screeches of overweight tires, we tooted our horn down the street—for once making an exception to the rule "no honking in Holland!"

We were on our way to another adventure. And we would never be the same.

Postscript

The Sharpe family returned to the United States and Norean resumed her teaching. Both children transitioned back into public schools and have now graduated from universities and embarked on careers of their own. Their Labrador Retriever, Mickie, passed away seven months after returning to the States, at the age of 15 years, 8 months, after a well-traveled life of romping through Alpine snow drifts and wading through warm Mediterranean water.

During the twenty years since their return, the Sharpes have seen their Dutch neighbors during numerous visits, both in the States and in Europe. Surprisingly, Norean has found multiple occasions to practice her Dutch with *Nederlandse mensen* who have immigrated to the United States and who are happy to humor her continued interest in their language and culture.

CPSIA information can be obtained
at www.ICGtesting.com
Printed in the USA
BVHW050450270522
638271BV00007B/138

9 781956 452044